Diana

Dream Big,

[signature]

What people are saying about Coach Burt

"Coach Micheal Burt is an exceptional communicator! He connects with the audience, delivers his message with passion, and creates an avenue for follow up on individual coaching needs with systems that work time and time again. I highly recommend Coach Burt for group therapy or one-on-one coaching."

—Jill Spry
State Farm Insurance

"Coach Burt is absolutely one of the strongest speakers we've ever had. He is one of the top talents, and we have a good eye for talent. I knew he was something special. He has taught us to go after bigger elephants, dream bigger dreams, have bigger hopes, and believe bigger things are possible. In 2009 I landed the largest account in our company's history. I do not believe I could have done it without Coach Burt."

—Rick Kloete
Senior Consultant, The Human
Capital Group

"From the moment I met Micheal I knew he was an industry transformer. From the way he thinks, responds, and sizes up situations to his deep knowledge of leadership, people development, and systems thinking, Micheal is unique and is a must-have for your company versus a nice-to-have. Micheal expands your thinking in ways you cannot imagine and sees unlimited possibility where others see nothing. Bring Micheal into your organization to coach, teach, or lead, and you will

see a drastic increase in your performance and the performance of your people."

—*Phil Cavender*
CEO and Founder
Cavender Financial Group

"I cannot thank you enough for a wonderful presentation! The
evaluation scores were the highest of any speaker we have ever
invited: 99.5 percent! Wow! I hear your 'words' spoken by the
social workers when I am in centers, and I see a change in their
attitudes and work. You helped them realize their value and the
leadership qualities that they have yet did not realize."

—*Hanna Clayton*
Regional Supervisor
National Healthcare Corporation

"Coach Burt brings new energy, new enthusiasm, new accounta-
bility, and new results to the table for us. I knew we needed
somebody, and he fit the ideal description with a background in
coaching and results. Our partnership has helped us refocus our
energy and efforts on what we can control daily and not make
excuses for those things that are beyond our influence."

—*John Floyd*
Ole South CEO/Founder

"Micheal has come into our organization to teach, grow, and retain
over 550 of our associates and to drive sales for us. His energy and
knowledge are contagious and have increased solutions to drive
people to us, increased our performance toward our ideal picture
of success, and personally challenged me to lead unlike any other.
The methodology we used helped us to achieve the largest increase in retail sales in the history of our company: a 43 percent

increase in 2009. If you are smart and you want to win in your markets, I would bring Micheal in NOW to get started."

—*Wib Evans*
COO, FirstBank

"Everyone needs to take stock in what Micheal Burt is preaching. His systematic approach to growing leaders helps companies to break through their current ceilings of success and experience breakthroughs. Coach Burt challenged us to lead and spent a good portion of his time educating us on the common dysfunctions of teams that served as roadblocks to our real potential. We are going to partner with Coach Burt in 2010 to continue to take us to new levels with his systems, his methodology, and his deep reservoir of knowledge that he garnered firsthand as a championship coach and now a championship business leader."

—*Shane Reeves*
CEO/Owner of Reeves-Sain

"Teaming up with Coach Burt in 2009 and putting his realistic approaches to generating new business helped FirstBank surpass management's wildest expectations. We opened 30% more checking accounts throughout our footprint and increased our retention of existing accounts by focusing on highly valued activities (HVAs) that attract and retain clients. We also noticed an increase of our clients referring their associates and friends to FirstBank effectively moving them from satisfied clients to FirstBank advocates. In the heat of competition, you always want proven leaders who'll help you attain your goals. Go with a proven winner & leader, Coach Micheal Burt!"

—*Chuck Lewis,*
Area President of FirstBank

"Coach Burt is a master motivator and a common sense communicator. His high energy, no nonsense approach is relevant and real. His sincere message comes from the heart and speaks to the heart. I highly recommend his very professional and powerfully positive presentation to anyone who wants to take their life to the next level."

—*Dan Schlafer,*
Tennessee School Boards
Association President

This
Ain't
No
Practice
Life

Other Books by Micheal Burt

Changing Lives Through Coaching

The Inspirational Leader

The Anatomy of Winning

This Ain't No Practice Life

Go from where you are to where you want to be

MICHEAL J. BURT

FRANKLIN GREEN
PUBLISHING

Brentwood, Tennessee

This Ain't No Practice Life
Published by Franklin Green Publishing
P.O. Box 2828
Brentwood, Tennessee 37024
www.franklingreenpublishing.com

ISBN: 978-0-98263-874-3

Layout and design: Sherry M. Wiser George
Editorial Assistance: Cathy Lower, Mitzi T. Brandon, Ed Curtis, Marc Pewitt
First Printing: June 2007, Maximum Success Publishing
Revised and Updated: July 2010, Franklin Green Publishing
For more information, visit www.coachburt.com

To all the people who I have met who desire to play at a different level in life and encourage me every day to dream bigger and manifest those dreams.

To my team headed up by Colby Jubenville, who won't stop until we go big time.

Mom: Thank you for the support and the unconditional love.

Wib Evans: Thank you for offering me the opportunity to drive results in the business world.

Lee Gessner: Thank you for becoming my publishing partner and seeing the value in my message and helping me to connect that message to many.

Donna Britt: Thanks for helping take *The Coach Micheal Burt Radio Show* around the world.

Contact Coach Burt today to book him for your next event!

CoachBurt.com
www.coachburt.com

4303 Pretoria Run
Murfreesboro, TN 37128

coach@coachburt.com
615.849.2099

Coach Micheal Burt speaks, coaches, trains, and leads individuals and organizations who want to play at a different level in life.

MAXIMUM SUCCESS
www.maximumsuccess.org

Maximum Success is a division of CoachBurt.com that focuses on speed and integration for clients in leadership, sales management, branding, and marketing.

Contents

Foreword

I FIRST MET MICHEAL BURT in the fall of 2007. We were introduced by a student he had coached in high school. This student was in one of my classes at Middle Tennessee State University. After class one day, the student said, "You should meet my coach. Ya'll are talking about the same things."

I teach like a head coach coaches football: speak the truth, block and tackle, and practice over and over again. If Micheal Burt coaches like me, I thought, he must be intense.

The next step in how we connected is a blur to me. I don't recall how he ended up in my classroom, but he did at some point. While he was speaking, I listened and caught the vision of the future that he was describing. At the conclusion of his presentation, I looked down at my paper and noticed that throughout my notes I had circled four words: voice, leadership, execution, and culture. In that moment my fate and future with Micheal Burt was sealed.

I walked up to him and said, "The essence of your message can be found in these four words."

He paused, looked up at me, and said, "O-k-a-y."

It was a long, drawn-out *okay* that gave him time to think. He looked at me for a moment and said, "Why don't we get together to discuss this further."

That's when our friendship was born. We have had countless meetings since then. We talk about dreams, failures, success, and the paths we are on. Each of those meetings has focused on dominant aspirations, identifying the strategies needed for success, and executing tasks with speed and integration.

In my car later I heard "Lose Yourself," by Marshall Mathers (a.k.a. Eminem). It reminded me of the essence of Micheal and the coachepreneur inside him. (A coachepreneur is what you get when you combine *coach* and *entrepreneur*.) The song's eerie melody lures listeners in and then poses a simple question that we all should ask ourselves: "If you had one shot, would you capture it or just let it slip?"

How would you answer that question? What if you woke up one day and could change the course of your life forever? Would you take that chance? Would you take that risk? Would you walk away from what you are currently doing and start chasing something that you believed was your calling?

We could ask a thousand people if they would like to chase their passion. How many do you think would actually do it?

How many people do you think would be willing to walk away from a career after they reached the pinnacle of success and then heard something inside of them say, "Go do something different"?

Just to make it interesting, assume that you spent a decade building your career to get to this point. Everything up to now has led you to this moment. What would happen if you felt yourself being pulled outside of your comfort zone? Would you consider walking away from the perfect opportunity you have spent your entire life working toward?

For the record, this perfect opportunity included your own gym, multiple championships, and the keys to the city. Would you leave all that behind?

Meet someone who asked himself these questions and then gave up everything he had achieved in order to try something new.

Meet someone who walked away after a championship season, followed his passion, and reinvented himself as a coachepreneur. You'll know what a coachepreneur really is after your first encounter with Micheal Burt. He makes you have conversations you don't want to have, do things you don't want to do, and become things that you never thought you could become.

If you spend a little time with him, you will easily see the difference between Coach Burt and other consultants who lead people to achieve objectives. Consultants know how to consult. Coach Burt knows how to win because he understands what very few people do. He understands the power of **collective passion**.

What is collective passion? We see it every day, but we don't spend much time pondering where it comes from. Collective passion is created by a unique relationship between an organization, its employees, and its customers. Collective passion is revealed in the brands we internalize, the experiences that we taste and touch, and management styles that inspire. In his book *Good to Great,* Jim Collins wrote about getting people on the right bus. But once those people are on the bus and in their right seats, you better have an engine in place that will move the bus toward its destination. For Micheal Burt, the fuel that drives the engine is collective passion.

It begins with a unique perspective. Seeing the world in a completely different way will allow you to try completely different things. Collective passion creates vested partners, people who have some skin in the game and are determined to succeed. Look closely at the people who Coach Burt works with. One thing that will stand out to you is the perception that Coach Burt's clients bring more knowledge, skill, desire, and belief to their business than their competitors.

At some point in life, we need to lose ourselves. We need to let go of the past and not allow fear of failure to hold us back. Reaching that decisive moment may be the result of events, inner growth, choices made over time, or because of an inability to make the right choices. Something inside Micheal Burt whispered and then screamed, "Its time for you to do more." Coach Burt calls that something *voice*. You'll get to know what that is, because while you are reading this book, you'll start to hear your unique voice grow louder with each passing page.

This book is a proven plan to reinvent yourself, your dreams, and your future. The question is, Will you do it or just let the opportunity slip away?

—*Dr. Colby B. Jubenville*
The Strategist

Preface

I BEGAN WRITING WHAT would become my greatest and deepest book in 2005, and I finished it in 2007 after winning a championship at Riverdale High School, a large comprehensive high school in Middle Tennessee. At that moment it represented my greatest professional achievement. *It was only the beginning.* Over the past five years I've been fortunate to help build winners from the inside out all across this country with a story of a small-town boy who seeks to squeeze all he can out of life. Now, I am fortunate to coach some of the top performing individuals and companies in the world and have part 2 of this story. The revised and updated version of this book represents what I've learned over the past five years through "Coaching Up Corporate America" and helping people to play at a different level in life.

Each of the decisions in this book is predicated by certain things that happen to us or that we create. Each of the decisions creates a season in your life, and if you can step back and see what season you are in, you can proceed to the next one. I did not know this when I wrote the book, but after giving the message to over 120,000 people, I have realized the true power of these seven decisions. I have more to add to the story. The revised and updated version of this book reflects the response people have given to me as a result of my message. I'm even more passionate today about the message than I was when I received the first copy of what would become my bestseller.

If you want to play at a different level in life, you've got to make a gut-level decision to go. You'll have to ask the hard questions, tackle the sacrifice I call the "cost of sale," and surround yourself with people who push you to the core. You'll have to find your unique calling through the your seven core decisions in intentional ways that quite possibly you've never done before. This will become a journey for you to become your best self and to tap into your unlimited potential. After all, potential is just kinetic energy that is stored until utilized. My philosophy is predicated on the fact that I believe everybody needs a coach in life to get their potential out of them. This coach is a person who affirms and validates your worth and potential in such a clear way that you begin to see it in yourself. If you've never had that, then you do now. It's time for me to help you unlock the kinetic energy that's been stored inside you for way to long. After all, we only get one life, but if we work it just right, one life is all we will ever need.

Enjoy the journey.

—*Coach Micheal Burt*

This
Ain't
No
Practice
Life

Introduction

MORE THAN NINE YEARS ago I began to speak to groups as part of my coaching profession. After a speaking engagement at a banquet one evening, a man came up to me and said, "You should really go on the speaking circuit because you have a true talent for speaking." His words lit a fire in me that continues to burn even stronger every day that I live. That day I begin to sense that God had given me a talent to inspire others with words and to light their fires so they could act on the hopes and dreams in their life.

Albert Schweitzer said, "In everyone's life, at some time, our inner fire burns out. That fire is then burst into flames by an encounter with another person, and we should all be thankful for those people who rekindle our inner spirit." I always use that quote to conclude my speeches.

As I continued to hone my craft of oration, I began to sense a much deeper hunger in my soul that said I was put here to help others find their voice in life. I began speaking at every opportunity and became a regular in a class at my alma mater, Middle Tennessee State

University. As I delivered my message in each class, I grew and began to realize the message I was delivering centered on four major themes: voice, leadership, execution, and culture. I began to title my presentation "This Ain't No Practice Life," a sentiment from a song I heard many years ago, called "Practice Life." I chose that title after my newly found premise that the ultimate success of one's life is measured by how he invests his time and energy in a cause that he deems worthy and significant and how much he impacts others along the journey.

Two years passed and my passion for inspiring a larger group continued to resurface, gnawing at my conscience and telling me there was a bigger world out there for me to impact. I was hungry to learn, and in the spring of 2003 I attended an Achiever's Circle offered by speaker and small business owner Mark Leblanc. My fire was reaffirmed and validated. At the end of that Achiever's Circle, Mark encouraged each participant to stand up and give three minutes of our best stuff. I was the youngest and most inexperienced speaker in the room, but I gave it all I had. When I had finished, I braced myself for the scrutiny and critical words of the other participants, especially Mark. He looked me squarely in the eye and said these profound words that stuck with me: "Micheal, if you don't write a book on that concept, it's nobody's fault but your own." Man, that was powerful, and it was exactly what I needed to grow my confidence and tackle the world.

Leadership can be defined in some circles as affirming someone else's self-worth and potential so much to them, in so clearly a way, that they begin to see it themselves. That day in 2003 I found my voice and knew deeply that I was here to help as many people as I can to find theirs. That's my mission in life and my deepest need for writing this book. Along the way I have met literally thousands of people who need an intentional blueprint to find their calling in life in order to become what they are capable of becoming. This is the book for you.

In the summer of 2004 I wrote my first book, *Changing Lives Through Coaching,* to help leaders formulate a vision for working with others and acting on that vision. It outlined my holistic approach to developing each member of my team from a body, mind, heart, and spirit paradigm and defined a method for tapping into the full potential of each constituent. I followed up with a spin-off entitled *The Inspirational Leader,* which outlined what I believed was a gap between how people wanted to lead and how they were actually leading and focused on leading others through inspiration and validation. Dr. Wayne Dyer taught me that there was a clear difference between inspiration and motivation. He said, "Motivation is where you have a hold of an idea that you take through to its logical conclusion. Inspiration is where the idea has a hold of you and it takes you to a place you intend to be."

I deeply enjoyed the writing process involved in both of those books. It was both therapeutic to me and, I hope, to those who read them. During that writing process I did exactly what I urge others to do, namely to connect with some of my passions in life and act on my thoughts. While I was engaged in the writing process, I knew I needed to address a greater theme, a theme for all people that was not limited to just coaches and leaders. That deep, burning desire led me to write this book and to reach out to as many people as I could. The word *inspire* means to breathe life into another, and ultimately that's what I think we are all searching for desperately.

Stephen Covey said, "Service is the rent we pay to live on this earth." Your situation may differ from others, but deep within your inner core is a longing to do something with your time and talent that matters, to find the sweet spot of your life. Every day you can choose to trade your time and energy for money or your talent and passion for purpose. From my experiences as a head coach of women's basketball, an athletic director, a speaker, and a consultant to people all across the United States, there are a few common threads that intertwine everyone. Those threads exist at one's deeper core of conscience, and they urge us to connect to our source, find our meaning and purpose, and live a life in service to people and causes in which we believe. The first step is to define a life well lived and daily work backward from that picture.

As I traveled the country speaking to virtually thousands of people in all walks of life on topics such as personal motivation, leadership, effective team building, and finding their passion, I found a common denominator: a need to live a life of passionate execution and significant contribution. People want to wake up in the morning with a sense of deep purpose that their lives affect others in a positive way and that they are connected to a cause they deem worthy. The other concept I've noticed throughout my travels is a gap between what people really want out of their lives and the results they're getting. What I've found between in the gap between that wonderful mental creation many people have and the physical act of creating it is usually a litany of excuses or perceived roadblocks. For whatever reason, people only act when there's enough pain or enough potential, otherwise they stay put and watch the days go by. Some say we will get twenty-five thousand mornings to awaken to in our lifetimes. I don't want to waste any of mine.

My hope is that this book will reach thousands of people and breathe life into them and give them the push they need to act on their thoughts and to truly write the program for their lives and, more important, live that program. I was speaking at a management seminar in New York when what I do for a living came to me. *I help people go from where they are to where they want to go. I illuminate and validate the potential in others in a clear way so they can begin to see it themselves.* Pretty simple, huh? But, boy, it's powerful when executed.

Anyone can make a living, but only the strong can make a life. What does your life represent? What is your purpose here? Don't you think it's time to begin the deep exploration into what you can become versus what you used to be?

I also found another common theme among people everywhere: We will all face some adversity in our lifetime. To what degree we face it will be unclear to predict, but how we use adversity to accelerate our progress will ultimately determine our level of significance in the world. In the end, between stimulus and response, YOU always have a choice as to how you respond. Some studies suggest that 50 percent of our happiness is born into us through our genetic codes. That leaves 50 percent up to us through what we feed our minds, who we associate with, and how we process failure. If you can change the picture of viewing adversity as a negative experience to one of learning, growing, and changing, then you can view bad situations as life's greatest teachers. In the Bible, the Word says that God is close to the brokenhearted. It could be that you're going through some adversity to humble your spirit and draw you closer to your Creator, and that ain't a bad thing in the grand scheme of things. In this book, we'll take a look at exactly how to use adversity to create intentional breakthroughs.

I want to challenge you. Today's the day to get off the mat, get rid of the excuses, and begin to build a life that matters. People don't regret what they do in life; they regret what they didn't do and what they're capable of doing. This book will include a road map to navigate you through life and help you get where you are going along this sometimes tumultuous journey. Follow the process, enjoy the ride, and promise yourself that you'll make every second count.

I've designed this book in a way that you can challenge yourself daily. The contents are built around *seven important decisions* and serve as the means to unlock *seven doors to your happiness and fulfillment*. I discovered these Seven Decisions while speaking to people from all walks of life. If you're not a big reader, take one challenge per day and make it a ninety-day process. By the end of the book, if you act on its content, I believe you will see a tremendous transformation in your life. The good and positive will begin to manifest itself in a way you have never experienced before, because all Seven Decisions are centered on taking ACTION.

To help illustrate my points I've included the Belief Model in the beginning of the book. It entails the processes of *Believing, Seeing, Doing,* and *Reflecting.* If you follow these keys, you'll begin to live your life by design versus by default and end up where you want to be on purpose versus by accident. You've absolutely got to decide today that you are the creative force for your life and that there's not one excuse out there that can stop you from truly living a life of deep meaning, passionate execution, and significant contribution. For you to truly make a major change in your life, you're simply going to have to take the time to stop and think.

Breakthroughs only happen when people stop and examine their underlying assumptions and realign the internal dialogue that is deeply scripted in their conscience with external actions. For the most part, what I've experienced in my travels is a profound misalignment between people's thoughts and actions, with very little time to stop, reflect, and change what they really want. Because of this cycle, people move in a direction they do not want to travel, because they are affected by people, environments, and other variables that leave them unsatisfied and unhappy. For any part of your life to change, you must first change.

At the end of the day, it's important to understand this simple concept: *this ain't no practice life.* Currently 41percent of all Americans do not have a living will. Apparently they believe they will live forever. Every day is crucial to living a life that matters. Every day you make four bets with your time, energy, creativity, and money. You always want to place those four in places that will yield the most return on your investment. No longer do you need only to think about the potential you have; you need to realize it. And the one thing you need to realize it is action. Talk is cheap. Now it's time to walk your talk and realize the power of your life!

As I write this book, I'm reminded of how much power words can have and how much they can impact others. I believe firmly that words can inspire and uplift, because that's what good books have done for me. As we begin this journey, I'm reminded of what William Faulkner said in his acceptance speech for the Nobel Prize in Literature:

> I believe that man will not merely endure: he will prevail. He is immortal, not because he alone among creatures has an inexhaustible voice, but because he has a soul, a spirit capable of compassion and sacrifice and endurance. The poet's, the writer's, duty is to write about these things. It is his privilege to help man endure by lifting his heart, by reminding him of the courage and honor and hope and pride and compassion and pity and sacrifice which has been the glory of his past. The poet's voice need not merely be the record of man, it can be one of the props, the pillars to help him endure and prevail.

My hope is that this writing will uplift and inspire you to work toward your dreams and to begin the process of self-discovery in search of your passions. The journey will be well worth the sacrifice, and the payoff will be immeasurable. The ability to unlock your sense of fulfillment by having the right keys is very satisfying and will improve your quality of life in every dimension.

Enjoy the journey!

Chapter 1

An Overview of the Seven Decisions

I THINK IT'S IMPORTANT to overview the Seven Decisions in the same order in which the book is outlined. The decisions are specifically positioned to go in sequential order, and if used properly, they will unlock the seven doors that will lead to more satisfaction and personal and professional fulfillment. I chose this terminology (decisions and doors) because I believe that we choose to open doors in our life at different times, but sometimes, for whatever reason, we are either not ready or do not have the essential skills to go through those doors. Many times we simply don't have the right key to open the doors. The roadblock may be personal or professional; it may have to do with internal or external factors, levels of maturity, lack of experience, lack of wisdom, or simply a timing factor. How frustrating is it to need to unlock a door to your house or car when you cannot find the right key? In our lives, not having the right keys is equally frustrating. This book will outline the doors that can be opened by using the right keys and will unlock the potential to the infinite future that you possess inside you that is just waiting to be unlocked.

THE SEVEN CORE DECISIONS

One Sunday I was sitting in the church in which I was raised, listening to my preacher, Herb Alsup. He began to outline five important concepts that would help one get to heaven. While I was listening, I realized that although life was messy and unpredictable, there were certain key principles that could help everyone improve, and if these were practiced, they could lead to a new level of advancement in life. The process would require belief, faith, knowledge, self-awareness, imagination, and most important, action. As Herb spoke, I fervently took notes and began to visualize some similar principles that I could share with audiences.

When I traveled, I began to see commonalities in what Herb said and what I was seeing all over the country. His words inspired me to come up with my own list of decisions that would lead to personal fulfillment. I labeled them the Seven Decisions to Play at a Different Level in Life, and I have shared them with individuals and organizations all over the country, roughly 125,000 people to date. If followed correctly, I believe these decisions will steer you toward some level of success. It is up to you to decide what that level will be. These decisions may appear obvious, but remember that sometimes what is common sense is not always common practice. Think deeply about each one, and you will begin to understand them at a deeper level, especially when you do the seven action items at the conclusion of each chapter. These will help you unlock your potential and live a life of deep meaning and significant contribution.

DECISION NO. 1: EXPERIENCE AN AWAKENING

Draw a Line in the Sand Between Who You Used to
Be and Who You Are Capable of Becoming

Friend, to get where you want to go, the first step is to confront the brutal facts about where you are currently. There is no fairy-tale world with fake trees and white elephants, but I believe a high percentage of Americans think they live there. When it comes to experiencing an awakening, you must first become highly proactive and take full responsibility for your lot in life. Your lot is yours, and you have created it by the decisions and actions you have taken up until this point. Not acting is really taking action.

You must begin to understand that we are where we are today because of the choices we have made up until today. In essence, we are the sum total of our decisions or lack thereof. Accept it and confront it and use the experiences that got you here as a steppingstone to the next level. Do a life inventory to see what is really going on with yourself. Check all your relationships, your vocation, your finances, your spirituality, your current limitations on your leadership style, and your potential and you will begin to get brutally honest with your success and failure in each one of those roles. You need to look in a mirror and decide that you will no longer live with mediocrity.

In *The 8th Habit* (2004), Stephen Covey wrote, "Everyone chooses one of two roads in life—the old and the young, the rich and the poor, men and women alike. One is the broad, well-traveled road to mediocrity, the other the road to greatness and meaning." He powerfully continues, "The path to mediocrity straightjackets human potential. The path to greatness unleashes and realizes human potential."

In his poem "The Road Not Taken," Robert Frost eloquently said, "Two roads diverged in a wood, and I, I took the one less traveled by. And that has made all the difference."

When you are ready to wake up, you are ready to realize that life is about so much more than just making it through the day. Life is no longer about just surviving and barely keeping your head above water; it's about thriving, completing projects, helping others, connecting, acting on a mission, and living. Life is about working in a vocation and doing something significant with your time and your talents. To discover your true voice, you simply have to start the process by WAKING UP!

When you experience this awakening. you draw a line in the sand that separates the old you from the new you. This line of demarcation is usually predicated by one of two things: pain or potential. One is a negative vision, and the other is a positive vision. But either way, it predicates some change in life. The next decisions will never happen in your life if you don't change your mind-set of reacting to what life throws at you to one of creating what happens to you.

DECISION NO. 2: DESIGN YOUR OWN DREAM

Get Intentional About Your Future

I firmly believe in Walt Disney's motto: "If you can dream it, you can do it." The beauty of America is that you have the freedom and the power to generate a vision in your head (mental creation), and no one can stop you from fulfilling that vision (physical creation). The poor can become rich, the unsuccessful can become successful, the small can become the big, and the underdog can become the top dog—if they only act on their visions.

People gravitate toward big thinkers, and the only way to truly tie yourself to a significant cause in your life is to think big thoughts and act on those big thoughts. We always attract back into our lives who we are. Remember, people do not regret what they do in life; they regret what they did not do. If life is about minimizing regret, then the quickest way to do that is to see a bigger picture and act on that picture. Between stimulus and response is a space, and in that space lies your freedom and ability to choose how you respond. If you live out of your imagination (infinite) instead of your memory (finite), you can begin with the end project in mind and work backward daily from that picture to create the life you envision versus the life you currently have.

In *The Structure of Scientific Revolutions* (1962), Thomas Kuhn said, "Every significant breakthrough that we've experienced in the world was first a break with an old thought pattern or paradigm into a new way of thinking." For you to live the life you want, you have to break with old, outdated thought patterns into new ways of thinking. Simply put: if you want to experience the success you've never experienced, you have to begin to think and act in ways that you've never thought before. There must be a break with the old into the new.

You will hear me say frequently throughout this book, "You cannot meet new challenges with old ways of thinking." The question becomes, "How do you expand your imagination to go beyond your own limitations in your mind?" In this chapter on dreaming we'll explore exactly how to get intentional about expanding your imagination. Dr. Wayne Dyer said, "Our greatest gift is the gift of our imagination." Nothing happens until something is imagined.

When you dream big, you create a world from your mind's eye, a world full of opportunity and potential so vast and unbelievable that you will feel as if there is just not enough time for you to accomplish all that you want to do in your life. You will approach every day with purpose and fervor and will see unlimited emotional power and endless possibilities. You will not be shackled by others' perceptions or limited in your vocation, and you especially will not be limited by your past. You will not accept no for an answer and will ultimately find a way to make your dreams a reality.

Remember, you've got the hammer and the nails to change your current perspective. Now go to work. When it comes to making money and dreaming, remember this simple concept that hit me like a ton of bricks one day while reading my horoscope: "Money doesn't grow on trees; it grows in the garden of your imagination. If you can dream it, you can make it." When you redefine what wealth means and replace financial wealth with happiness and fulfillment, you begin to dream big versus small, and life is about a mission, not a paycheck. Many times if you chase being the best in your vocation, money will simply chase you. Start the process today by becoming intentional about your dreams.

DECISION NO. 3: LEARN TO PLAY UP

To Get Better You've Got to Get
Around Those Who Are Better

If you want to get better at anything you do in life, you've got to learn to play with people who are better than you. Many people never do this because they always want to be the biggest fish in the pond. Eight out of ten times, if a person walks like a winner, talks like a winner, dresses like a winner, and acts like a winner, he's a winner.

Statistics tell us that you have exactly thirty seconds to make a positive first impression, and if you drop the ball here, it will take twenty-one positive interactions to overcome that first bad impression. Dennis Waitley said that people make a decision to explore what's on the inside of a book by depending on its outside. He wasn't referring to expensive clothing, but rather a warm, inviting spirit and how we connect with others. To be successful, dressing up simply does not do it. But getting rid of the toxins in your life—energy drainers, clock eaters, and negative forces—will be a big step in the right direction.

If you want to be world class, then you've got to carry yourself and treat others as world class. Every time you speak, you are projecting and affirming to others how they should treat you. You have an opportunity daily to add or subtract value from the lives of others, and likewise they have the same opportunity over you.

When you begin to live from a paradigm of wholeness and goodness, you operate from a moral compass that others can feel and see. You pull yourself out of activities that could detract from your reputation or perception and begin to associate with people who believe in your own worth and potential and lift you up rather than tear you down. You operate from a perspective of abundance, not scarcity. You see life as an adventure in the exchange of meaning and positive energy with others. You forgive those who have transgressed against you. You realize that we are all wayward travelers who face the same struggles in pursuit of the same thing: meaning and happiness.

One component of cleansing your life is to be loyal to those who are absent by not discussing them negatively behind their backs. "If you want to retain those that are present, be loyal to those that are absent" (Covey, 2004). Being loyal to those who are absent builds a strong brand of integrity for those both present and not. People will secretly respect you more if you do not undermine others when they are not at hand to defend themselves. This bad habit stems from insecurity and manifests itself from a scarcity mentality paradigm. The abundance mentality teaches us that there is enough for everyone to have all they want; we do not have to badmouth others in the process to get what we want. We make ourselves look inferior when we resort to trashing others. Secure people do not gain confidence from making others look bad. They build up others or confront those with whom they have challenges, and they do it in a way that is respectful and balanced, between courage and consideration (a strong sign of emotional maturity).

Trust flows from trustworthiness, and it can only be gained by making big deposits into the emotional bank accounts of others on a continual basis. Through this process of deep investment, one can truly transform the lives of others. Start today by cleaning out the trash in your life. Be loyal to those who are absent, and be happy for the success of others. Petty jealousies only make you look weak and inferior and cast a glimpse into your soul. Illuminate means to shine light on darkness. So illuminate others every chance you get. It will come back to you tenfold. Cleansing your life and marrying your internal intentions with your external actions creates "intentional congruence" in your life. You will be lining up your conscience and your actions, giving you not peace of mind but rather peace of conscience.

As you begin to clean your life up, you will begin to realize the benefits of continuing your education. I don't mean you have to go back to college, but you should constantly be engaged in educating your mind, your heart, and your conscience. From this continual process will flow opportunity and the ability to see situations from multiple dimensions, which will actively expand your circle of influence and build you into a commodity the world needs.

You should be hungry to learn, because this process of education builds both intellect quotient and emotional intelligence and makes you marketable to the world. As you grow your skills, you will discover that there will always be a place for your talents in the marketplace, effectively making you an asset in the workforce.

In today's volatile markets you need hard skills versus the traditional lines people use to win that focus on personality, such as people skills. Today, you need hard skills such as the ability to sell, to solve problems, to do technical work, or to add tremendous value through your unique contributions based on your unique past and experiences. This deep understanding alone unlocks the doors to opportunity and helps you to fully comprehend that you never have to go to a job you don't love—NEVER.

You choose what you do for a living. In essence, you never trade your time and energy for money, but rather your talent and passion for purpose. Without education or training, you may limit the opportunities you have. But with that training, you will open more doors than you could ever handle. Each step of my educational journey I have only opened more doors, and I know the single greatest driving force behind that is continual learning. If you don't currently like your lot in life, go back into the education process until you become a solution to what the world needs and will pay you to do.

Every action we take is driven by our thoughts, and our thoughts are no wiser than our understandings. To drive new actions we must first widen our understandings, and we do this by cleansing our life of the things that hold us back and by beginning to play up those that challenge and coach us. I will walk you through finding your voice in life, which includes making major decisions about what you do for a living to meet the financial realities of your life. It all begins with a period of evaluating your current life and removing things and people who push you to new levels!

Decision No. 4: Make Learning a Way of Being

Decide Today to Become a Lifelong Learner

Knowledge is all around us, just knocking at our doors and trying desperately to get in. We have been repeatedly trained our whole lives in how to speak, write, and communicate, but we have had less than two full weeks of training in how to listen. We have two ears, two eyes, and one mouth. With these we can hear and observe twice as much as we speak, but we don't always follow that adage. When you listen to others, you are given a window into their soul. They are trying so hard to tell you how they feel, what they are interested in, what they stand for, what they are passionate about, and what they need from you. To be an effective person personally and professionally we have to listen and make a fundamental decision to make learning our way of being.

Successful people observe and listen to everything around them, and they make a concerted effort to listen to and learn from the great minds of their day. They feed their spirit with information that sharpens their saw in all dimensions. They get in a regular habit of growth and development. Years ago, for the first time in my life, I was able to see and meet in person my greatest leadership mentor, Dr. Stephen Covey, author of *The Seven Habits of Highly Effective*

People (1989). I listened with my head and my heart intently and searched for the deep meaning he was offering. I tried to be a disciple of his work so I could effectively influence others from the principles he was teaching.

If you want to be great at anything, open your heart and mind to the vast knowledge of those around you and practice empathic listening: the practice of listening from another's frame of reference instead of your own. You are trying to feel where they are coming from, and for a moment you trade perspectives with them and walk in their shoes. You listen from a dual perspective and act accordingly. If you want to be successful, then listen to the words being spoken. Listen with the intention of truly seeking to understand rather than reply. Open and communicate with your heart and your soul. Seek first the benefit of others and listen to their stories and hear their songs. This will build compassion in you and allow you to become a light to others who may desperately need it. This will also build and educate your conscience, which will serve you throughout your life.

Another facet of learning is the forming of your own board of directors, a group of concerned and knowledgeable lifeline people who can help you negotiate life's struggles and opportunities. This personal board of directors should meet with you at least twice a year to offer guidance, both personal and professional, to you as you navigate the uncertain waters of life. Their expertise will offer wisdom, guidance, and support in emotional and tough times in your life.

I saw not long ago a saying that a good life is a series of good decisions. It then asked how you make good decisions and answered that good decisions come with experience and wisdom. How do you gain experience and wisdom? Well, by making bad decisions. As you educate your conscience in the differences between right and wrong, you learn to be calm and quiet and simply listen to your internal voice. Many times that voice will lead you exactly where you need to be and away from where you don't.

To play at a different level in life you must make a key decision that says you will become a lifelong learner in multiple disciplines in your life. We will tackle specific ways to embed daily learning into your life until it becomes part of your DNA. One of the top strategies I used when I was a women's basketball head coach was to weave life and wisdom teachings into the fabric of my organization that communicated to my team that I was more interested in their becoming winners in life rather than just on the court. If you engineer people to win, they'll produce what you want them to produce. This begins by making intentional learning an everyday event in your life and the life of your organization.

Decision No. 5: Add Value Versus Subtracting It

Every Day We Have an Opportunity
to Add Value to Others

The price in life must always be paid, and the process must always be followed. There are no shortcuts to success. The law of the harvest certainly factors in here. More and more we are seeing how important relationships are in our lives. We seldom get intentional about building, strengthening, or acquiring new relationships, and in many interactions, we don't add value to those in our life, we subtract it. Would you ever dare to plant a garden and not water it, not offer it any sunlight, and expect it to be successful? Your life and relationships are exactly the same way. We water what we want to grow. In your life you must "garden your garden" and tend to every aspect of it if you want to be successful. In this chapter and with this decision we focus on how to always add value versus subtracting it. The great preacher Dr. Charles Stanley said, "We always reap what we sow, more than we sowed it, for longer than it was sown." In essence, what we tend to and feed into other people will always come back more and for longer than we sowed it.

The second part of adding value versus subtracting it is the concept of paying the appropriate price for success. I refer to this as the "cost of sale." In the financial world a strategist will tell you that if you want to play at a certain level financially, it will cost you a specific amount in order to be productive. In life, the cost of sale will be the sacrifice you make and the price that must be paid in order to arrive at your desired outcome.

Be weary of the get-rich-quick scheme or the wealth-without-work approach. Anything worth having in life has to be earned. With growth sometimes comes pain, but you can begin to see adversity as an accelerator to your progress, not stagnation to your movement. If viewed from this perspective, you approach the inevitable obstacles of life with grace and dignity, not as deal breakers to your future.

The law of the harvest governs life, which teaches us that nature and we are one as a "living system." Living systems are governed by natural laws or principles that are self-evident, timeless, and universal. When we neglect these principles we suffer the consequences. Think about how nature operates on its own timetable that cannot be rushed. Success is the same way. It is a journey of exploration and inquiry into life.

Mohandas Gandhi said that seven things would destroy us. If you take the time to study each very slowly, you can see how the law of the harvest is violated in each deadly sin:

- Wealth without work
- Pleasure without conscience
- Knowledge without character
- Commerce without morality
- Science without humanity

- Worship without sacrifice
- Politics without principle

Each of these things can be obtained with false actions, although the percentages are very small for you to really reach wealth without any work. The other six can be instrumental in your demise if you avoid the real cost. The key lies in your ability to pay the price in order to reap the benefit. For every action in our life there are reactions from both the world and others. These reactions usually flow from predictable patterns. The natural consequence of your not being trustworthy is that others choose not to trust you; the natural consequence of your paying the price is that opportunity is afforded you. Once you understand this process, you understand that everything is exactly as it should be at this moment in the world.

For salespeople, I use Newton's law—"An object (person) at rest will stay at rest unless acted upon by an outside factor"—to explain why it is important to touch prospects seven to fifteen times to convert them into clients. Many times people don't act unless they are encouraged to act. You can be the driving catalyst of change in their life if you give them a nudge. Poor salespeople rely on the market and luck to win, but seasoned professionals act within their circle of influence to drive results.

Many times in life you reach a certain level, similar to climbing a mountain. You believe you are at the top when you reach a certain peak, but the reality of the situation is that when you get to that rise, you are only at a level to see so much more than before. Paying the process will be exactly the same way. You'll reach certain points where you believe you have made some major progress only to see so much more of life when you get there.

I believe that with each year you live you continue to expand and grow. With each day of learning, you expand your horizons. Your mind and experiences will never regress to their earlier dimensions.

Like a muscle, your brain gets stronger the more you utilize it, but it atrophies when you don't utilize it.

Successful people who leave lasting impressions on society and in organizations are continuous learners who constantly pay the prices of studying, reading, teaching, and growing. They seek new material like they seek air to breathe. They see life as an upward spiral of continuous growth. With each circle they get better and better and "sharpen their saw" (Covey, 1989), knowing that by "sharpening their saw" they become an asset in the world that others need. They always compete on experience versus commodity. They truly add value to their life and everyone they touch. The person who pays up is solutions oriented, not problem oriented, and he or she obtains the skill set and tools necessary to transcend any marketplace.

As you pay the price of significance understand that there will be rocks down life's gravel road. It's not what happens to us that hurts us; it is ultimately our response to what happens to us that does. Understand that there are ultimately three options as offered in Collins (2001) *Good to Great* in a study by the Center for Victimization. This study focused on individuals who suffered major adversity, ranging from cancer to automobile accidents. The three responses included people who were permanently disabled by the event (they did not recover), those who just got their life back to normal, and those who used the event as a defining moment for their future success. Think about how you handle adversity. If you're going to add value versus subtract it, you understand that heartache will certainly be some of the cost of doing business. Use that as a way to build character in your life and as a wellspring of inspiration for yourself and others.

Part of adding value is the process of growing your influence. This process is one of constantly working at the outside edge of your circle of influence by taking initiative and showing others that you are a catalyst for positive change and growth. As you make and keep your commitments to others, you see yourself growing in both influence and responsibilities in the workplace and in the community as others begin to respect you in ways that only affirm the your worth and potential. This new influence taps into your conscience's need to connect to something larger than yourself. This process is very liberating to the soul and solidifies you in the world as you begin to make positive improvements to the world and with the people with whom you interact. In this chapter we focus on specific ways for you to add tremendous value to those you interact with and to create a mind-set of building advocates and promoters for life.

DECISION NO. 6: BUILD UP VERSUS TEAR DOWN

Leadership in a New Era

Zig Ziglar said, "If you help enough people get what they want in life, you'll get what you want." I totally agree. As I get older I have begun to get so much satisfaction from building others up versus tearing them down. When you build others up you affirm their self-worth and potential so much that they truly begin to illuminate it in themselves. You should seek every opportunity to affirm the worth and potential in others just as great leaders have done for you. As you begin to see the good in others, they will begin, like a mirror, to reflect the good in you as well. The key to the many in life is the one. Build relationships one at a time in your personal and professional lives. Invest time and energy in order to ignite others' fires and watch and see how it manifests in your life. When you reach a certain point on the maturity continuum you begin to understand and fully realize that you have the ability to have tremendous influence in the world.

I mentioned earlier my encounter with Dr. Stephen Covey. He flattered and built me up by signing a copy of his book and writing that I was a Trim-tab, which is a metaphor for one who uses his power of influence to affectively change the lives of many. A trim-tab on a boat or ship is the small rudder that turns the big rudder that turns the entire vessel. These people can move themselves and their teams or departments in such a way that it positively affects the entire organization. A Trim-tab exercises high levels of initiative within his or her circle of influence until that circle expands exponentially and disciples are created. We could all be trim-tabs in any situation because leadership is a choice.

Successful people look out the window to give credit to others when things go well, but they look in the mirror to accept blame when things go wrong (Collins, 2001). When you build others up, you connect your heart and spirit's need to leave a legacy of your life, and that can only be done by thinking beyond yourself. Every significant contribution in the world was done by and with others.

The reality of the situation is that we live in an interdependent society, and the only way the world will ever survive is through this concept. This goes against the grain of the deep scripting and hardwiring in our lives to look out for Number One and to always push our agendas at the expense of the group. When I ask people how many classes they had in school in leadership, how to be a good teammate, or how to articulate their own value and contribution to the world, the common response is none. We drastically underprepare people to work in team environments, but we put them on teams in the workplace and can't figure out why this doesn't work. It doesn't work because we've never been taught the hard skills to be good teammates or how to function in the context of good teams. It explains why there are so many bad teams in the world.

We must build others up and not resort to scarcity mentality thinking, where we constantly tear others down and get caught up in confessing the sins of others. Look for golden opportunities to have crucial conversations that connect to others that will put money in their emotional bank account versus withdrawing it. Seek daily to build up as many people as you can, and watch how they return that kindness and courtesy to you. "Be a light, not a judge, be a model, not a critic" (Covey, 2004). Start today by BUILDING UP all those you come in contact with. I'll teach you my Target 25 strategy and introduce you to my Legacy Management System to build a personal network that will drive long-term relationships that add value in both directions.

DECISION NO. 7: ACT OR BE ACTED UPON

Between Thinking and Doing Is a Space

In *The Greatest Salesman in the World,* Og Mandino (1982) said, "My goals are worthless, my plans are impossible, and none will be of any value unless followed by action." Each of the first six decisions will take you nowhere unless you have the self-discipline to act on them. The word *discipline* is a derivative of the word *disciple,* which means to give yourself to a person or cause in which you believe. You are the only person who owns your future because you're the only person who can see it in your mind.

The execution gap between thinking and doing across this country is mind-boggling. So many people just think and talk but never connect the dots to the most important phase of living a meaningful life around action and execution.

If you knew that you had only six months to live, would you be so hesitant to act on your dreams? Would you be hesitant to build up others? Would you be so consumed with working every second of every day? Would you get so irate about the minute things in your life? Would you take for granted those important souls who have come into your life for a reason? My guess is no.

At the top of my personal mission statement are four words: Passion, Patience, Persistence, and Perseverance. I believe you need these four attributes to live a life of deep meaning and significant contribution. At the bottom of that mission statement I added the most powerful mission statement of all: Live like you are dying. If you were to live like you were dying you would most certainly ACT versus be ACTED upon. You would reconcile every situation in your life that was heavy on your heart. You would forgive every person who has transgressed against you. You would work each day with passion and meaning and would look for golden teachable moments to make a difference in the lives of others. You would see time for exactly what it is: the most precious commodity you have. You would not be so caught up in material things, petty arguments, insecurities, jealousies, and the success of others. You would truly operate within your circle of influence to use your time and talents wisely. You would live life to the fullest. You know the best advice I could give you today:

Go live like you are dying.

In this chapter I offer important information that ninety-five-year-olds shared while laying on their deathbed about what's important for us today. When we begin with the finished product in mind for our lives, we begin to act in alignment with what matters most to us today so we can do something tomorrow that we simply can't do today. In this regard we minimize regret by acting on our hopes and dreams.

THE PROCESS OF UNLOCKING THE DOORS:
THE BELIEF AND ACTION MODEL

To execute the Seven Decisions and unlock the doors to your potential you need to follow a sequential process, which is illustrated in Figure 1.1. This model was developed through a discussion with a friend and fellow businessman while on a speaking trip to Eastern

Tennessee. The conversation focused on manifestation and the challenge so many people had with taking thought and turning it into action. The model begins with believing that it is possible for you to have anything that you want in life.

Without belief, your dreams are dead in the water, and lacking confidence (the memory of success) keeps so many from manifesting their dreams. From this belief stems a vision or seeing of what you want. I call this an itch or future pull. This seeing has not yet manifested, but is the seed of the fruit you are going to produce. This is the mental creation: seeing the world through the mind's eye. From the mental creation, action must be attached in order to see results. Always remember, not all thinkers are achievers, but all achievers are thinkers. Unfortunately people breakdown either in the belief stage or in the action stage, which prohibits them from ever fully realizing their potential.

In an effort to achieve results you need to focus on growing yourself in four key areas: knowledge (for the mind), skills (for the body), desire (for the heart), and belief (for the spirit). Any fragmenting of these four dimensions will result in another failure to realize your potential and will stagnate and stifle growth toward bringing your vision into manifest.

My friend Tony says that there are two types of manifestation that occur in our lives. The first is intentional manifestation, where we intentionally co-create something happening in life. We believe it can happen, we visualize it, we act on our vision, and we reflect on what we accomplish. This book operates primarily from that paradigm. The second form of manifestation is unintentional, where things emerge in your life as a result of connection to your source and conscience. We refer to this as "mysterious manifestation." This is an interesting phenomenon and one that we will explore in another book.

Once you go through the first three parts of creating results in your life, it is vitally important to stop and reflect on those results to see what worked and what needs to be changed in order to build future capacity. If you do not do this, because we are creatures of habit, we will constantly repeat the same patterns without ever realizing why we keep getting the same results. This reflection challenges you to see how your actions affected both you and others, and it encourages you to move into an age of wisdom, an era I think we are in today.

The model of manifestation is similarly centered on a three-step process in the personal aspect: knowing, dreaming, and being. From the professional perspective we know the process to be: knowledge, imagination, and manifestation. For the purposes of this book we will use the following model titled the Belief and Action Model.

The Belief and Action Model

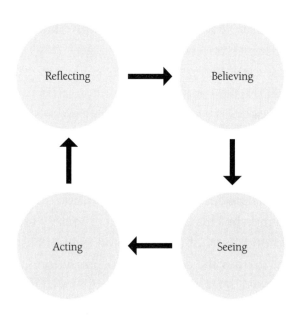

Chapter 2

Experience an Awakening

DRAW A LINE IN THE SAND TODAY

I THINK EVERY PERSON should wake up in the morning with a purpose and a reason for living. Progress toward a destination you want to reach will serve as one of the strongest motivators in your life. Knowing where you want to go is the first step. Many people spend more time planning their vacations than they do planning their lives. To do this you must first come to a very strong realization. Your time and energy are the most precious commodities you will ever have. How you choose to spend and invest your time—as well as with whom you spend and invest your time—determines your quality of life. In this section I want to open your eyes to how most people spend theirs.

What if I told you that the average person spends 23 years sleeping, 9.5 years in their car, 6 years eating, 1–5 years in religious activities, 6 months to a year at red lights, 140 days making and unmaking your bed, 15–20 years in some form of education, and (here's the kicker) 35–50 years working. Now how important is your time? Also, 70 percent of all people don't like their jobs. The average person spends 12 to 14 hours per day working just to get through what's on their plate (let alone do anything significant or important to them); 88 percent say it's hard to balance their personal and professional lives. An average person receives 6 voice mail messages per day, sits in 1.6 meetings that 85 percent say are unimportant and 88 percent say had absolutely nothing to do with the mission of the organization. Now how important is your time?

My point is this: there is no such thing as time management. Can you speed up, slow down, or stop time? The key is to awaken to the point of marrying your time and energy with the highest value of that time and energy toward the dominant place you want to go. Success is intentional, with focused energy toward a destination versus wasted energy with no purpose.

At many of my workshops across the country, people want to know how they can better manage their time. The point is that you can't. You don't manage time. You spend it with the people you care about, you invest it in things and people you deem worthy, or you flat out waste it. It's that simple. The key to managing your time is to decide what is most important to you (quality of life) and place those things, people, and activities in your allotment of time.

Experts say that we will awaken to twenty-five thousand mornings. You must make a conscious decision not to waste any of yours. Many times the people I work with allow things, agendas, and work schedules to dominate their life. They take the approach of victim, but that couldn't be further from the truth. You control your life, and you certainly control how you invest your time. Don't ever let anyone tell you any different.

Think about this. If I were to give you $86,400 this morning and told you that at midnight you lost any money you didn't use, that it did not carry over to the next day, what would you do with that money? Typical answers I get are spend it, invest it, or waste it. Those are all good answers. We all know people who spend the money they have on the people they love. We all know some people who waste the money they have. If you don't believe that, then study the number of people who go bankrupt after winning a huge lottery jackpot. We also know people who might invest the money to build future capacity. The key here is this: we all have something far more precious than $86,400 per day. We have 86,400 seconds per day. My guess is that you still fall into one of those three categories: you're spending it with the people you love or in causes you deem worthy, investing it with the people you care about through wisdom and teaching, or you're flat out wasting it.

Smart people try to spend and invest their 168 hours per week in activities and with people who make them happy and fulfilled. It's also vitally important to have a nice balance between your personal and professional lives. If you get all of your satisfaction off the job or on the job, then it's time to evaluate the quality of the things you're placing in your time in other areas. An integrated life is a whole life, not a compartmentalized life where you segment parts with no correlation to each other. Because of the number of hours spent in a job, we need to redefine the role of that job within the context of a bigger picture, how that job is tied to a bigger future we want to manifest.

Now that you have a better understanding of how people spend their time, you need to understand that every day you make four bets with yours. Mark Leblanc, owner of *Small Business Success* and the biggest person who influenced me to write my first book, says, "Every day you make four bets: your time, energy, money, and creativity." I agree. What goes into your time in those four areas will ultimately come out on the other end. Be a poor planner and steward of that time, and you will most likely one day regret you didn't do something meaningful with yours. Remember, we minimize regret through action, but prioritizing how we should spend our time puts us in alignment with the highest value of that time.

There are two simple models you can use when it comes to your life. Organize, act, and evaluate or continue, stop, and start. These are simple concepts that pay enormous dividends. Living effectively is a continual process of adjustments based seeing needs and filling needs. You do this daily. Remember, "Where there's no gardener, there's no garden." So always water what you want to grow. Think about how much you're tending to your garden.

As I discuss the importance of planning the use of your time, it is vitally important to know and connect to your mission in life, and to do that, you need a mission statement or defining statement. I'll discuss this later under *Decision No. 2: Design Your Dream*. As you begin to grow yourself in the four key areas—knowledge, skills, desire, and belief—you build capacity to accept full responsibility for your life and your actions around how you spend your time. Remember, quality of life begins with how you choose to spend or invest your time. Most of the successful people I know accept full responsibility for their life and do not blame the past, the environment, or others for how they choose to live.

OWN THE ACTIVITY AND THE RESULTS

At the heart of the term *proactivity* is accepting FULL responsibility for your lot in life. It means that you have the power to choose your response to any situation you encounter in life, that you can take the initiative to change the way you see any situation instantaneously, and that although you may predisposed to certain genetic, psychological, or physical factors, you are not determined by them. My point is simple: YOU ALWAYS HAVE A CHOICE! The positive of recognizing this is that you can change anything in your life if you want to. As you begin to practice mindfulness and grow your self-awareness, you hide from nothing and you accept both positive and negative thoughts and circumstances in your life. You bring an awareness of what is actually going on. Through self-awareness (the ability to reflect on your life as you live it), imagination (the ability to create a better world in your head), independent will (the ability to act on what you want to change), and conscience (a sense of right and wrong), you can change.

Bad habits are like the strong pull of gravity hauling you right back where you don't need to be. To break these bad habits you first have to acknowledge them and accept the truth as it is. You will not be able to meet new challenges or garner new successes with old ways of thinking and old habits. Out of all the people I coach, sometimes the task is most difficult with the ones who have had the most success. They cannot check their past success and become past focused versus future focused. All your best days should be in your future, never in your past. Remember, to make a new contribution to this world and to your life, you must create a whole new preparation. An old preparation simply will not create a new result.

As you begin to understand this powerful concept, you move away from becoming the opposite of proactive, which is reactive. Reactive people blame others for their lot in life, make excuses when they don't get the results they want, and spend their lives disempowering themselves and allowing the weaknesses of others to control them. Reactive people go negative the first time something goes wrong and very rarely want to accept responsibility for anything, unless it's successful.

Every day you either work *in* your business getting new business or *on* your business improving your current business. To get anywhere you want to go you must focus on two important things: activity and results. There will never be any results without activity. The question then becomes, Is the activity tied to the highest value of your time toward where you want to go? If it's not then it's a low-level activity and most likely a waste of your time.

Victor Frankl, author of *Man's Search for Meaning,* noted while being severely mistreated in a Nazi prison camp that no one could take away what he called his "Last Human Freedom," which was the power to choose his response to virtually any situation in life. Between stimulus and response (see the diagram below) is a space, and in that space lies our ability to choose.

Stimulus ➡ Response

To live a life of deep meaning and significant contribution in service to others we must develop the capacity or self-discipline to ACT within that space. The only lasting form of discipline is self-discipline, but that discipline must be cultivated by winning the private battle over one's moods or feelings. We are not our moods and feelings, although many times we succumb to both of them. The term *sacrifice* means to subordinate what you want now for what you want later. It is only when we accept full responsibility for our life and completely understand that we have a choice in all situations that we become responsible for our lives, and then we make the shift from reactive to proactive. In that space we revert back to our deep scripting, hardwiring, and software (environment). To create a new response we must first examine our underlying assumptions about any situation.

When you take this responsibility you will gain a deep level of freedom. It will be emancipating and liberating to take back control of your thoughts, your beliefs, your vision, and your actions. This freedom will release you from the self-imposed prisons of blaming, criticizing, contending, comparing, and allowing others' thoughts, actions, or words control your life. You will truly be set free and understand that both your confidence and value are not predicated on what others think about you but rather what you think about yourself. How does a beautiful woman let a man control how she feels about herself? Between stimulus (his words) and her response (her confidence and counter to his words) she disempowers herself and allows him to control her. Always remember that you own your activity and results, not anybody else.

THE LINE IN THE SAND BEGINS BY TELLING THE TRUTH

One of the hardest things we'll ever have to do is to confront the brutal facts of our lives while at the same time never losing faith that we will reach where we are going through consistent, repetitive, deliberate action. When you confront the facts about where you are and where you want to go, you begin to expose weak areas in your life that quite possibly you have neglected for years. In the end, the process will be of far greater value than the product, and we must always value the journey along the way. Struggle is where the most memories and the impact of others will take place in life.

The easy thing to do in life is to live in a nonreality, to not want to confront difficulties, insecurities, shortcomings, or failures, but they are essential steppingstones to success if viewed properly. Drawing a line in the sand allows you to engage in a set of new and consistent behaviors today that allow you to do something tomorrow you simply can't do today. The payoff will be well worth the sacrifice.

Confronting the brutal facts means not living a lie and owning and accepting who you are and what you've done (no matter how it affects how others perceive you), recognizing mistakes and transgressions against others, and moving to a place of peace and harmony. We must all realize that we are where we are today because of all the decisions we made up until today. As we become vulnerable and understand that we all have challenges in our life, we understand that we do not have to conceal those vulnerabilities but only embrace them and work to improve them.

Many people judge others based on a snapshot or decision that was made in the past. This snapshot does not represent where you could be today, but is only reflective of where you were at one time. Don't judge others based on their snapshots. Understand that your past is not who you currently are unless you continue practicing those old behaviors.

This means we have to create relationships with others, both personally and professionally, where the truth is heard and facts are given. Too many times we sugarcoat what is actually happening to our friends and co-workers, and that leaves them with skewed facts to work from and inaccurate paradigms to reflect on. As we become vulnerable and confront the facts we must NEVER lose faith that we will move forward. In *Decision No. 5: Add Value Versus Subtracting It,* I will discuss using adversity to accelerate progress in your life, but you can only do this if you accept the situation as it is (not filtered), take responsibility for the situation, and work with a focus, faith, and passion to change the situation.

Dr. Phil McGraw says, "We can't change what we won't acknowledge." This is the step of acknowledgment that is critical to turning the wheels of change. Confront where you are today and have unwavering faith that you will get where you are going. This vision, seeing the world through the mind's eye, coupled with discipline, will help you use the facts to create the world you want versus being a victim of the one you're currently in.

COMPLETE A TOTAL INVENTORY OF YOUR LIFE: GET REAL

"The history of free man is never written by chance but by choice—their choice."—*Dwight D. Eisenhower*

I've got the ultimate questions for you and I want you to look in the mirror and not out the window for the answer. I want you to get real serious, confront the brutal facts, and increase your self-awareness so that you can give yourself an honest answer to these questions. The most important conversations in your life will be the ones you have with yourself. Isn't it about time to start having the life you really want? Isn't it time to have the career you want, drive the car you want, be in a relationship with the person you want, associate with the friends you like, go to church where you want, get involved with the project you want, volunteer like you have been talking about, lose the weight you want to lose, build the house you want to live in, and live the way you want to. Folks, it's past time. No longer should you make excuses of fear of failure, laziness, insecurity, fear of embarrassment, lack of self-discipline, the activity trap of life, or whatever you want to place between your knowing what type of life you want to have and you actually creating it. It's time to understand that this ain't no practice life.

Ponder these words from ninety-two-year-old Gordon Hinckley:

I am no longer a young man filled with energy and vitality. I'm given to meditation and prayer. I would enjoy sitting in a rocker, swallowing prescriptions, listening to soft music, and contemplating the things of the universe. But such activity offers no challenge and makes no contribution. I wish to be up and doing. I wish to face each day with resolution and purpose. I wish to use every waking hour to give encouragement, to bless those whose burdens are heavy, to build faith and strength of testimony. It is the presence of wonderful people which stimulates the adrenaline. It is the look of love in their eyes which gives me energy.

What do you wish to be doing today? In high school one of my toughest and most challenging teachers, Barbara Parker, who is now director of schools, asked us to do an exercise where we basically wrote out the life we would like to have. At the time we didn't fully understand the exercise, but in its essence it now carries tremendous power. I wrote all the things I wanted to do with my life as if I actually did write that program. After grading the paper she returned it to us with a very strong question. In bright red ink on the back it said, "Then why aren't you doing it?"

Only 3 percent of the people in this country write out their dreams, and guess what: those 3 percent usually manifest their dreams. It wasn't until years later that I fully appreciated that question back in high school and believed enough in it to share it with you. If you were to write down the life you really wanted to live, including the career you wanted to have, the house you wanted to live in, the relationship you wanted to be in, the community member everyone appreciated, the family member you aspired to be, the friend you would like to have, the true person you wanted to be, the car you wanted to drive, the vacation you'd like to be on, and on and on, what would those things say?

My question to you is, Why aren't you doing all of those things with your life? You do have control over it, don't you? We get one ride on this merry-go-round, and your choices are simple: live a life of design or a life of default. My advice to you is to choose wisely.

By taking an inventory of your life right now and consistently reflecting on how you are choosing to spend your time, you can make decisions based on what is most important versus simply what is momentarily urgent. If you're not careful, urgency and activity traps of life will drive all your time and leave you unhappy and unfulfilled. An effective person wakes up, consistently studies where he spends his time, and makes the necessary adjustments to live life by design (you create it) versus default (other people or circumstances create it).

To complete an inventory of your life, you must fully embrace where you are. Several years ago, while I was writing my first book, *Changing Lives Through Coaching,* I created a maturity continuum that offered a picture of where you could be today. If you locate yourself on this continuum and don't like where you are, don't worry. We can always change it. Here are the five levels of people:

Category 1 (Reactors): You are a reactive person who responds after the fact to whatever life throws at you. You wake up in the morning with little or no direction and float through the galaxy, dodging bullets and just trying to survive. If you're in this category, leading yourself or other people will be very difficult. After all, how can you lead others when you can't inspire yourself? Reactors typically complain about their lot in life and blame a host of others for their failures. They live their life as a function of other people's weaknesses or circumstances that they believe they have little control over. They're the opposite of proactive, which at its core means to take full responsibility for the success or failure of your life. A Reactor's failure is never his fault. Bet you know or work with a whole host of those!

You must focus solely on your circle of influence to change the things in your life that you are reactive about. Reactors very rarely get ahead in life, because they usually waste the precious time they've been given. If you're in this category, we need to light your fire immediately and help you to understand the importance of connecting to an important mission and being forward looking. Don't let your past hold your future hostage. The unfortunate part of most Reactors is that they have developed a functional blindness to their own defects. They can never see themselves as reactive, so that thought limits their awareness and ability to act. As we grow our knowledge, we also grow our ignorance. I know it's a paradox, but really intelligent people understand that the more we know, the more we don't know. Until we become humble and teachable, we can never fully grow and get better. This self-awareness will either propel our growth or limit our progress.

Category 2 (Strugglers): You know what you want to do with your life, but you don't know how to get it. You haven't paid the real price for success or invested in the education or training necessary to thrive in today's global marketplace. You have not gardened your garden and know it deep down. Remember, you must water what you want to grow. You may have the vision but lack the discipline and passion to execute the plan to achieve success. Because of this reactive planning, you become frustrated and intimidated and think success is out there only for the lucky and the strong, and you don't perceive yourself to be in either of those two categories.

Remember this: ALL the successful people in the world started somewhere, and many of them began from less than glamorous situations. If you don't believe me, just watch the hundreds of episodes of any biographical show that outlines a star's rise from virtually nothing. Decide today that you are going to be one of those people, and let's get you started. Struggling equals you being paralyzed because you have limiting perceptions. Change the picture and believe in yourself, because others won't until you do.

If you're in this category the key word is *belief*. You see, confidence comes only from the memory of success, and success can only be achieved by consistent, repetitive practice. If you want to move out of the struggling phase, act over and over again until you feel confident that you can do it. If you want to stay right where you are, try one time, let it not work, and become frustrated and intimidated. This guarantees stagnation and complacency. Unfortunately some people live in complacent worlds and only complain about them.

Category 3 (Thinkers): You know what you want, you know how to get it, but you are caught in an activity trap, the business of life, and you just can't get started on those hopes and dreams. These are the "Someday" people. Next year I'll improve or be the person that I envision. I just can't right now because I'm so busy. There are certainly no guarantees for tomorrow, and the last time I checked, today is the most important day of your life.

Leadership expert John C. Maxwell says, "Yesterday's a cancelled check; tomorrow's a promissory note, so today is the only day that really matters." The first step on the path to greatness is to overcome inertia.

You've got all the tools, so go for it. My motto is, "There's only one way in life to profit, and that's by taking a risk." The only real risk is riskless living. Stick your neck out and remember that you'll miss 100 percent of the shots you don't take and miss 100 percent of the dreams you don't pursue.

The next time you have a great idea that you are passionate about, write it down and then act on it. Two thousand people might tell you it's absurd, but if my memory serves me correctly, that's how many times Thomas Edison tried to invent the light bulb before it worked. Consider it a two-thousand-step process. The next step on the maturity level that follows creating a vision is creating the discipline and passion and having a properly educated conscience to execute that vision. If you're a thinker, we're headed in the right direction, but the equation is simply incomplete until you act. We've got to connect more of the dots in order to have a happy ending.

Category 4 (Floaters): You know what you want, you know how to get it, and you go out into the real world to try it, but you fail for reasons in and out of your control. As a result, you become cynical and pessimistic about the process and just stay right where you are. Your failure reaffirms that you knew you couldn't attain your goal, and your shortcoming is only proof of your nonexistence and shallow thinking. Folks, the going rate for any worthwhile win is ten setbacks. The tenth try might be the trick, and all the others could be unanswered prayers. Only time will tell, but you're sure to fail if you feel sorry for yourself or think that people always get it right the first time. I've been rejected for several jobs, and all of them have turned out to be blessings in disguise. I'm sure you've got your own list of what seemed to be a disaster at the time only later to find out that what happened was one of the best things that ever happened to you.

If you fail a number of times, get in line with the millions of people that do so every day. Learn from it and move on to the next opportunity. The right fit will certainly come along sooner rather than later if you focus on your circle of influence and keep improving your skills. Harvey Mackey's book *I Got Fired and It's the Best Thing That Ever Happened to Me* outlines several successful people who were fired along the way. When adversity hits, ask one simple question: What is this trying to teach me? I'll outline ways later in the book to actually use adversity to accelerate progress in your life versus allowing it to become debilitating and paralyzing.

Category 5 (Doers and Achievers): You are the movers and shakers of the world. The average person can't keep up with you because the word *average* doesn't fit into your language system. You are proactive, self-disciplined, have enormous amounts of emotional intelligence, have found your voice in life, and are on your way to living a life of deep meaning and significant contribution. Smart people will do one thing: harness your potential and let you go. They will get out of your way and let you work. A smart leader will hire as many of these people as possible, because they will build enduring organizations and make lasting impacts on others. You will be disappointed occasionally to find out that some people just don't get you and can't figure out why you can't just be stagnant and quit trying to improve everything. The truth is that most of those people want to be like you and can't stand that you are making things happen.

Expect a lot of resistance from many of the people you come into contact with who absolutely are scared to death of change and may not be as intrinsically motivated as you are. Don't let them stop you or slow you down. Just ask them quietly to get out of your way. You keep on keeping on, fight the good fight every day, and know that you are doing something that matters. You are proceeding in an upward spiral of improvement toward your hopes and dreams.

Doers and Achievers are the people who make a significant difference in the lives of others. They leave unwavering legacies in organizations that will never be forgotten. They truly understand the difference between transformation and transaction.

Dr. Phil McGraw became increasingly popular with millions of people across the world when he used the term "Get real" about your life several years ago. I believe that we all at times fall into predictable categories that I've outlined in my Five Levels of Life. You can move up the ladder to where you are a Doer and Achiever. Most people have the latent and undeveloped potential to move up the food chain, but they just have to have the initiative and educated conscience to do so. Real significance is harnessed at the fifth level, so your goal should be to continuously move up the ladder of success.

Not long ago I was curious about becoming intentional with happiness. Most people equate success with being happy, so I began studying what truly makes people happy. Most psychologists believe that each of us has a happiness set point where 50 percent of our happiness is born into us in our DNA, 10 percent of our happiness lies in who we associate with, and 40 percent is determined by what we feed our mind, how we process failure, and our perspectives on life. My point is simple: if you're interested in getting happy, begin to confront the brutal facts about what's causing your unhappiness and start becoming intentional about your happiness just like you are about your work goals.

For a great read, pick up *The Happiness Project* by Gretchen Rubin (2009) and start your own twelve-month plan to get happy. You'll be glad you did.

PRIVATE VICTORIES PRECEDE PUBLIC VICTORIES

The toughest battles you will ever fight will be the internal struggles you have between what you're doing, and what you should be doing. Some refer to this as "creative tension," which is the gap between your current reality and the future reality you wish to create. Conscience, if educated properly, drives our decision making if we only listen to it more often. I'll discuss the importance of listening to your still, small voice later in *Decision No. 4: Make Learning a Way of Being.*

As you begin to grow your emotional muscles and build your capacity to make and keep commitments to yourself, you will then grow your capacity to meet the needs of others. Part of the process of finding your own voice is developing the ability to make and keep commitments and promises to yourself. When you do more of this, you begin to break down old habits of lack of execution and begin to build new internal muscles that help you meet the challenges of a permanent whitewater society. The emotional tension and anxiety of not translating thoughts into action will evaporate, and you will view the creative tension between current reality and hopeful reality as energy that will promote positive change. Change in life many times is a result of either pain or potential. The tension actually creates action, which is what is needed to break through in life.

When you lift weights you experience a certain pain. That pain is prompted by the breaking down of muscle fibers that then rebuild themselves and become even stronger after your workout. You must first meet the challenge, go beyond past limitations, and then work to go into new arenas of success. This process is the equivalent of building the emotional strength to build the capacity necessary to meet whatever comes your way. Only when you have paid the price to personal victory will you be able to have public victory. If your life is flawed with internal conflict and your own inability to make and keep promises to yourself, you will never be able to lead others or serve in productive ways, because your friends and colleagues will detect this duplicity from your actions, and your trustworthiness will be negated. Private victories could be as simple as not being negative about others behind their backs, getting up when you said you would, working out like you said you would, or following up with someone when you told them you would. Win the private victory and the public victories will begin to show.

Isn't it time you connected with your unique gifts in life?

Finding your unique voice in life will be one of the most important journeys you'll ever take. Detecting this voice (your calling in life) will begin the process of unleashing the enormous talent and potential inside of you and will awaken the passion to move to the next level in your life where you can then begin to inspire others. It is the equivalent of developing your gift in life and giving it away to as many people as you can. Stephen Covey said, "Service is the rent we pay to live on this earth," and the key to the many is through the one. We have a hard time serving others when we have not found our voice.

When I speak about this across the country I am amazed at how many people have never begun the process of discovering their voice and therefore have lived in self-imposed prisons of jobs as occupations versus contributing in careers as vocations. As we reflect on how we invest our time, we begin to understand that a quality life revolves around a holistic approach that taps into our four birth gifts: body, mind, heart, and spirit. Unfortunately our education system is not equipped to help us find this gift by asking the right questions and helping us to hone the gifts we need that are in alignment with our highest self. Follow the needs of each of these endowments and see where you are lacking:

1. The body's need is to live and meet the economic realities of the world. This would be PQ (physical intelligence).
2. The mind's need is to learn, grow, and expand. This would be IQ (intellect quotient).
3. The heart's need is to love something or somebody and to be loved. This would be EQ (emotional intelligence).
4. The spirit's need is to connect to something larger, to be a part of something meaningful, to contribute. It also has a need to

connect to conscience and act in thoughtful ways to human kind. This would be SQ (spiritual intelligence).

In essence this model represents a four-dimensional paradigm for finding your voice in life. To break that down would mean that most people have a deep need:

1. To live (body)
2. To learn (mind)
3. To love (heart)
4. To leave a legacy (spirit)

As we explore this Whole Person theory introduced by Stephen Covey (my favorite author), we begin the process of finding our unique voice by tapping into our body, mind, heart, and spirit. As we find that voice, here are some specific questions:

1. What are you deeply passionate about?
2. What could you be the best in the world at?
3. What drives your economic engine?
4. Where can you fulfill a need in the world by marrying your unique talent with your passions in alignment with your conscience, or need for meaning?
5. If you have found your voice or calling in life, how can you drive your talents into a niche market that you can dominant, where clients can only get what your selling through you?

SIMPLE WAYS TO DETECT YOUR VOICE

The Process Is Just as Important as the Product

As we travel through our life we begin to get excited about things even to the point that we become obsessed with them. They light our fire, they give us causes to wake up for in the morning, we deem them worthy of our time, and we give our whole self to being good at them. That's our passion, and that's where we need to be investing our time. I am frequently asked, "How do I figure out what I'm passionate about?" Or someone says, "I think my passions are evolving." I think both are perfectly legitimate. Let me give you a couple of simple ways to find and detect your passion, because I truly believe, when we're deciding how to spend our time, passion has to be involved.

Passion is the emotional fuel that drives the engine of success. Be sure you fully understand, contrary to some speaker's words, that passion is not some overused quick-fix buzzword. It may be underdone and underdeveloped, but people need to be talking about passion all the time because it's the gas that drives your engine. Without it, life is dull and mundane. We need passion in our jobs, relationships, hobbies, and virtually everything we do. If you are trying to detect your passion, then ask yourself these questions:

1. What would I drive all night through two states to talk about for free in the morning to five people?
2. What would I work at for forty hours a week for free if I knew it would lead to peace of mind, happiness, financial freedom, and fulfillment in the long run?
3. What do I get excited about when I talk about it?
4. What could I spend hours researching on the Internet?
5. What do I truly love at my core?
6. When somebody is doing something for a living that I would like to do, what is that?

When you begin to answer those questions, you'll begin the process of finding your passion. It is feasible that your passion will evolve over the years. I began as a basketball coach trying to win games, and I have evolved into a person who wants to influence millions of people. My passion has evolved from coaching basketball players to developing leaders and influencing people to do something significant with their life and solving challenges for companies around the world. Find your passion, do it for a living, and you'll never work another day for the rest of your life. Once you answer those questions you are on your way to choosing a vocation that will bring significance to your life. If you have children, one of the single greatest things you will do for them will be to help them detect their unique gifts in life.

UNDERSTANDING THE DIFFERENCE BETWEEN OCCUPATION AND VOCATION

The Difference Between a Paycheck and a Significant Life

I believe it is vitally important to mention here the difference between an occupation and a vocation, because the legacy our lives are tied to will most likely be made during our careers. When one chooses what his craft will be for a living, it is vitally important to create synergy between passion, talent, needs of the world, and conscience. Remember, the body has a need to live, the mind has a need to learn, the heart has a need to love and be passionately involved with a worthy cause, and the spirit has a need to leave a legacy in life. If any one of these areas is neglected, then an imbalance will occur, resulting in unhappiness and lack of fulfillment.

By finding your voice after asking the questions above, you can choose to be involved with a vocation. This word stems from a Latin root meaning "voice" or "calling" in life, which offers you an opportunity to become a disciple of a cause or project you believe is worthy of your time. Occupation simply means that which occupies your time for which you receive a paycheck. Now which would you really like to have? An occupation or a vocation?

Instead of trading your time and energy for a paycheck, you should trade your talents and passion for purpose and hopefully a paycheck will follow. I tell people to chase being the best at what they do, and money will chase them. If you chase being mediocre at what you do, then mediocre money will follow. The bigger the contribution, the bigger the reward. Part of practicing the concepts in this book challenge you to look inward and explore your latent and undeveloped gifts, find those gifts, and give those gifts away during your transactions with others. When your work, play, and love all intersect, then you've got passion, and that's an irresistible belief for motive and action.

Now is the time to decide what you want your vocation to be and quit just making it through the day by going to an occupation. Remember, your voice is your gift in life, and that gift is so valuable that it must be risked and given to others. By hoarding your talent you are ensuring that it will never be used, and there is no tragedy as great as an unopened gift. As you study the following diagram, think about these five questions. I believe that they hold the key to unlocking your future significance:

1. What are my latent talents?
2. Where are there needs in the world that people will pay me to fulfill?
3. What can I be a part of that taps into my conscience, my need for meaning, and my desire to connect to something larger than myself?
4. What am I deeply passionate about?
5. What drives my economic engine? How much money do I need to make to meet the realities of my world?

Finding Your Unique Voice at the Intersection of the Five Circles

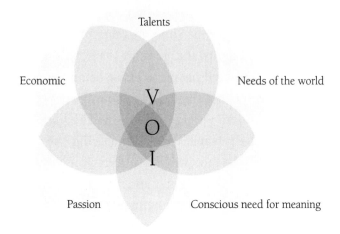

As you go through this model, its contents will be validated by helping you to find your voice at the nexus or intersection of the five circles. Not long ago, I re-took this test while I was traveling back from a speaking engagement. There were certain areas I needed to re-fine, but for the most part I figured out that I had found my voice. This gave me tremendous satisfaction both personally and professionally to know that I am involved in projects in life that pay me fairly (body), treat me kindly (heart), use me creatively (mind), and tap into my conscience for meaning (spirit).

Now that you know how to detect your voice it's time to begin the process of intentional manifestation in your life by creating your life.

THE BEST WAY TO PREDICT THE FUTURE IS TO CREATE IT

The final key to open the door to responsibility and self-awareness in your life is to understand that the best way to predict your future is to create it. By building your capacity through self-discipline, becoming proactive versus reactive, by taking an inventory of your life, and by finding and detecting your unique voice in life you can then become the creative force for your life. Your fire will be lit by your passions, and you will fully understand that we only get one life and what we do with it solely rests within our circle of influence and control.

Once we grasp this powerful concept, we begin to work at the outside edge of that initiative to grow our influence and begin to move in a powerful direction in an upward spiral of improvement and growth at an unstoppable pace. We are internally driven to succeed, no matter what. We then take full responsibility for our life and realize that if we want to create a better life for ourselves, then we must create that life through intentional manifestation. From this perspective we write the book of our life and have the power and capacity to live from that book. We have two options: live our lives by design or live them by default.

One of the most difficult challenges we will face will be the ability to act in a way that we have already predetermined in our head around our core value system in times of stress or pressure. In my second book, *The Inspirational Leader,* I wrote that being the person at the end of the day that we set out to be in the beginning is an enormous character builder. When we create this synergy between our walk and our talk, we begin to cultivate integrity in the totality of our life, which represents wholeness and goodness. An integrated life is not compartmentalized, but whole and integrated as one. Success in some roles of our lives does not mean we can be failures in other roles.

The most difficult aspect of leading will be to tell yourself that you want to lead one way only to have the many daily stimuli of environmental conditions push that person out of being. The same principle applies to waking up and fully grasping the concept that you are in charge of yourself. No other person can make you feel a certain way, facilitate a bad mood, change your mind, treat you poorly, or decide your success or failure in this world without your specific consent. Once you begin to operate from this paradigm, you can drive your own boat.

I use the boat analogy because, as I write this, I'm on an Alaskan cruise. If you could only see what I see, you would want to wake up and take full responsibility for your life, because you would understand the immense benefits of taking control of your own destiny.

There are only a few reasons why people don't attempt to create their future. Here are a few:

1. Fear of failure—which stagnates growth.
2. Not enough faith in the end—which creates hopelessness.
3. Fear of the work involved—which causes boredom and stagnation.
4. Afraid of the journey—which causes life to become dull and mundane.
5. Lack of education—which creates atrophy in the brain.
6. Limiting beliefs most likely instilled during primitive years.
7. Reactive to the negative pull of the environment surrounding them.

As I've worked with people in all parts of the world I've used the body, mind, heart, and spirit model to accurately diagnose and prescribe most of the ills people face personally and in the workplace. Just take a moment to reflect on what happens when:

- For the body: You are not paid fairly to meet the economic realities of the world. Or you do not take care of your physical body and you cannot perform at optimum levels.
- For the mind: You are not used creatively, you don't challenge your mind, you don't grow, and you allow yourself to fall victim to atrophy and stagnation.
- For the heart: You are not treated kindly, you do not project love to others, and you are not passionate about the causes you involve yourself with.

- For the spirit: You do not believe in the mission of what you are doing, you've been dispirited by events, or you have lost faith in the messenger or the message.

The clear result of these violations of our four parts manifests in these ways:

- For the body: You seek additional jobs, you moonlight, or you become lethargic and stagnate, which leaves you empty and unfulfilled.
- For the mind: You daydream, you become dull, you become obsolete in the market, or you check in and pick up a paycheck but do not commit your true intellect.
- For the heart: You withdraw yourself to protect, you become disengaged, you lose your passion, or you just quit altogether.
- For the spirit: You become dispirited, lost, broken, and you lose all faith in the mission of what you are doing.

As you can see, violating any of these four dimensions of whole people will result in profound misalignment of conscience. This disconnect will eat at your soul. This places an enormous emphasis on finding your voice in life and creating balance in all its dimensions so that you are living a life that really matters to you and to those you associate with. To manifest these actions, begin by practicing these important decisions and watch your own credibility with yourself grow and expand exponentially.

Chapter 2 Summary: Seven Action Items to Manifest the Decision of Experiencing an Awakening

1. *Today,* I will plan to use my time wisely with people and causes I

deem worthy. I will value the time I have been given and not use any energy toward negativity or areas that *waste my time*. I will begin planning and executing that plan so I can translate my mission into the daily moments of my life. I will realize that if I know and fail to do, then I might as well not know.

2. *Today,* I will accept full responsibility for my life, my thoughts, and my actions. I will think only in terms of how I can improve, how I can affect the situations I face, what I feel about others, and how I can contribute to the greater good. I will accept my lot in life and not project blame on others or my past for where I am today. Today, I will chose to become proactive rather than reactive to the pressures of life. I will view life as a journey and an adventure filled with continuous learning.

3. *Today,* I will no longer run from the facts of my life. I will confront them in their totality. I will accept the fact that it is what it is and will operate from an environment where the truth is heard. I will listen to my internal voice when seeking guidance, and I will connect to that conscience. I will understand that wherever I am today is not permanent, only temporary, and I will have unwavering faith that I can and will improve and prevail. I will work with strength from a higher source that teaches us that everything is exactly as it should be at this moment. Today, I will understand that people are perfectly aligned to get the results they are getting in life.

4. *Today,* I will take a serious inventory of my life in all dimensions— body, mind, heart, spirit—to see where I currently stand. I will ask hard questions, such as am I taking care of my body through consistent, repetitive exercise? Am I engaged in continual learning and sharpening of my skills? Do I practice love and work from a passionate perspective in the causes I associate with? Am I connected with my source and do I believe in what I'm doing? Once I take a hard

look at my life, I will then form action plans to make the necessary changes to get the results I want.

5. *Today,* I will begin the day by getting out of bed when I said I would. I will win the daily private victories by keeping my commitments to myself and others. I will not participate in saying anything negative about another person for the entire day. I will set goals and achieve them without wavering, because I believe deeply in their contents. I will educate and obey my conscience by continually seeking to refine my knowledge, skills, desire, and belief.

6. *Today,* I will think deeply about finding and detecting my voice. I will ask the questions mentioned in this chapter and take a hard look at my present situation. If I have not found my voice or I am in an occupation, I will seek areas of the job I am passionate about or I will look at other professions that create a synergy between body, mind, heart, and spirit. If I have found my voice, I will search for opportunities to give away that voice to others and will help and inspire others to find their voice. I will value teaching opportunities to impart wisdom and knowledge to those I touch and seek to transform rather than transact with them.

7. *Today,* I will understand that I am the creative force of my life. I am the writer of the program, and I can live that program by design rather than by default. I will no longer allow others to define me and will not worry about social status, the pride of being right, or how others portray me. I will work from a strong belief in what I'm doing toward a destination I deem worthy. I will no longer waste my time or talents in causes I do not believe in and will work within my circle of influence to do good for the world. I will connect to my deepest mission and purpose with a fire that will inspire and uplift all those I associate with. I will become a creative force that drives good and change in the world.

Chapter 3

Design Your Own Dream

SEVEN WAYS TO INTENTIONALLY MANIFEST A NEW FUTURE

"If one advances confidently in the direction of his dreams and endeavors to live the life he has imagined, he will meet with success unexpected in common hours."

—*Henry David Thoreau*

DREAMS REALLY DO COME true. From the time Christine Clifford was a young woman, she wanted to be an author. Throughout her youth she cherished writing assignments and looked forward to journalism duties in college. When she was sidelined by life circumstances, she chose to go into the business world and quickly rose to become a senior executive vice president of an international marketing company.

In 1994 Christine was diagnosed with breast cancer, a cancer that had spiraled her mother into a deep depression years earlier and caused her father to leave. Christine was determined to use this adversity to accelerate progress rather than stagnate movement in her life (*Key No. 5: Pay Up*). Four weeks after her surgery, she awoke in the middle of the night with a vision—cartoons. From there she began reading intently whatever was available on humor and cancer, but there was very little. So she wrote *Not Now, I'm Having a No Hair Day* and *Our Family Has Cancer, Too!* Both books became very instrumental in using humor to alleviate the devastation and mental anguish that accompanies cancer. Christine eloquently said, "Today is a good day to dream." Why should you put off dreaming until tomorrow when you could live out of your imagination today? That imagination will lead you to a better life as long as you break away from the old and into the new.

—*Paraphrased from* Chicken Soup for the Writer's Soul *(2000) by Jack Canfield, Mark Victor Hansen, and Bud Gardner*

LIVE OUT OF YOUR IMAGINATION INSTEAD OF YOUR MEMORY

"A journey requires opening doors that are shut, walking in dark spaces that are frightening, and touching the flame that burns" (Kouzes and Posner, 2002). The question becomes can and will you dream enough to challenge you to go beyond where you currently are? The mind can be transformed. Paulo Coelho wrote, "Each thing has to transform itself into something better and acquire a new destiny." You see, the brain stays elastic throughout life, changing itself as we begin to challenge old habits. Studies show that the brain has a quarter of a second, called a quarter choice point, in which to catch old, destructive habits before acting on them.

We have been granted an unbelievable, unique human endowment that animals do not have: imagination. Our imagination allows us to create a better world in our minds than what we currently have. As you begin to live out of your imagination, you start to see the infinite possibilities of what you could become versus the past conditions of your life or your present reality. For some reason, too many people allow their past actions or circumstances to hold their future success hostage, and I am just not buying it. As I look out over the Pacific Ocean while traveling along the Canadian coast, I see no boundaries, no limitations, and certainly no fear. I only see unlimited opportunity and infinite possibilities. I see miles upon never-ending miles of ocean and air. Your life carries the same possibilities: unlimited opportunity.

As we become continual learners (*Decision No. 4: Make Learning a Way of Being*), we begin to see opportunity everywhere, and we constantly think about ways to improve both our lives and the lives of those around us. We see possibilities, not limitations. Every experience in every venue is viewed as a learning experience that gives us more tools, more skills, and more knowledge to build an ever-increasing reservoir of knowledge that can be used at every stop along our journey. The only way to expand our imagination is by two intentional acts: education and experience. We are limited only by our ability to see a bigger future in our minds that is directly related to our past scripting.

To break through the tiny pictures, we must continually be exposed to those who have broken through to new levels of experience. This comes through constantly educating our minds and hearts. Wayne Dyer said, "Imagination is our greatest gift." Nothing happens until something is imagined because the process of manifestation in your life is twofold: first, mental, and then physical. To create a new contribution in life you need a new preparation. You'll have to see it first with the mind's eye and then add specific, ongoing, repetitive action toward your dominant focus to create that which you see.

One common denominator that I see among people across the country is that they have created self-imposed prisons and have not grown their imaginations. They are trapped, limiting both their happiness and success, and they just can't figure out how to get out. They continually think inside the box, and they have begun to believe that there is nothing bigger for them. This self-imposed prison keeps them exactly where they are and stagnates future growth. They have created the very adversity they disdain in their own lives. They want more but have sold out their dreams and simply settled for their current lot in life.

Let me set you straight: our time on earth is much to short to just SETTLE for anything in any compartment of your life. It is time you start to think big and act on those thoughts and use the key of imagination to unlock the door to your prison of the past actions. Go act on those dreams and move in the direction of your imagination and watch what happens. Expect lots of resistance and adversity throughout as the natural pull of some people in a scarcity society is to hold you back rather than propel you forward. With every dream there will be a cost of sale. In essence, this is the price or sacrifice you will be expected to pay to reach where you want to go.

If you truly want to expand your imagination, get around people who think bigger than you do and start doing three things per day toward where you want to be. We'll call these three things High Value Activities, because they combine the highest value of your time toward your dominant focus of manifesting what you want in your life. Three per day, five days per week, will create sixty things per month. Before long you will begin to see progress toward that picture in your head. Remember, there are no unrealistic dreams in life, only unrealistic time frames to reach those dreams.

Sometimes we get so caught up in the activity traps of life and just churn out whatever it is we churn out that we seldom take any time to really think about our lives. Sure when we see something that moves us or we listen to someone who inspires us, we do a quick reality check of our situation, but then we seldom act on our thoughts. We think about it for a while and then revert back to our old patterns of thoughts and actions because they are comfortable. *A comfortable*

Design Your Own Dream

> **IMAGINATION ASSIGNMENT**
>
> Take two minutes and think about the life you really want
> and the specific high value activities you can do
> to manifest that life (Dream Up).
> **Live out of your imagination instead of your memory.**

life leads to a mediocre life. If you were to take just two minutes of un-interrupted time right now and think of the three to five things in your life (or more) that you want to change, what would they be? Have you done a life inventory lately to see if your life is headed anywhere?

I believe people are perfectly aligned to get the results they are searching for in their lives. Aim low and you will reach it, aim high and you will reach it. My challenge to you today is to live out of your imagination instead of your memory. What you used to be does not matter, because the past is finite and the present and future are infinite. Michel Angelo said, "It's not that we set our sights to high and miss, but we set them too low and we hit."

What you can be does matter a great deal. The first step on this journey of self-discovery is figuring out where you are today and understanding this. Albert Einstein said, "The significant problems we face today cannot be solved at the same level of thinking we were at when we created them." One definition of insanity is to continue doing what you are doing and expect different results. If you want to change something in your life, you must go to a new level of thinking and, more important, a new level of doing!

To go, you must first paint a picture in your head of where you want to go (imagination) and what type of life you aspire to have. You must create a vision of seeing the world through your mind's eye. "Vision is applied imagination" (Covey, 2004). William James said,

"Most people live in a very restricted circle of their potential being. We all have reservoirs of energy and genius to draw upon of which we do not dream."

I am sure right now you can see yourself lying on a beautiful beach with your significant other (the one you like) and reaping the benefits of all of those great things you have worked so hard to attain in your life. Paint the picture for your life and begin to live from that picture. Without a picture of the person you could be, chances are you will stay the person you are or what others or society defines you to be. Remember, if you always do what you have always done, then you will always get what you have always gotten.

Get the picture? If you do not create a vision, everything will look exactly the same ten years from now—with maybe some added pounds. This process starts by writing down your dreams. Only 3 percent of the population write down their dreams, and those are the 3 percent who create the life of their dreams. To live beyond your wildest expectations, you've first got to have some wild expectations, and this begins with imagination.

NEVER LET YOUR PAST HOLD YOUR FUTURE HOSTAGE

We have all done things in our past of which we are not proud. We all have. "When it's all said and done, people will far more regret what they didn't do with their lives than what they did with their lives." You may be embarrassed by what you have done. You may not want to replicate it, reproduce it, or relive it, and that's fine. But it was a learning experience, and that is all. If you allow something that has happened to you in the past to hinder your thought process, stop you from acting, or keep you from achieving any future success, then you have effectively disempowered yourself and allowed the past to hold your future hostage.

Folks, the past is finite, which means it cannot be changed. It is over. The future is infinite and holds unlimited opportunity. So many future opportunities are held hostage by our regret and guilt over the past. We should be concerned with using our past experiences to build better futures and our wisdom from our failures to help others navigate life's tough waters, but we should never let it define us. Past decisions are just snapshots of our lives. Sometimes we are not proud of those snapshots, but they were instrumental in getting us to where we want to arrive. I sincerely believe that we are moving into an age of wisdom. Our goal should be to package those snapshots in our suitcase of wisdom and take them with us. Wisdom helps us navigate the rocky streams of life because of past experiences. We learn, we grow, and we help others through our own successes and failures.

If people are still judging you based on something that happened in your past, it is their problem, not yours. You don't need those people anyway, because they were never really on board with you. We live in such a fickle society that yesterday's good friends could be tomorrow's enemies. If you truly cultivate deep relationships with others, sometimes you will be disappointed by their actions and decisions, but if you mistrust them you'll be miserable and suspicious all the time. Mature people accept others for who they currently are and what they can become, not what they used to be.

The societal push to judge people based on their past is simply an immature and shortsighted way of thinking. What if all your future accomplishments were put on hold because of the things you did in the past? What if you were judged today based on where you were ten years ago? You wouldn't like that, would you? I know I wouldn't. Who I am today is not in any way who I used to be, and you are exactly the same way. Every day our knowledge grows and expands, and we should never go back to our past dimensions. It is the beauty of life: the ability to re-invent and re-create ourselves in new ways based on new learning experiences. It is almost impossible to go backward unless by conscious choice.

Make a choice today that you will no longer allow anything you have done in the past to define your future potential. Separate where you are today, no matter how low that is, from where you could be. There are countless examples of people who went from nowhere to somewhere because they dreamed and acted. Be one of those people—nothing should be holding you back.

The Zen garden of Kyoto has an entry gate referred to as *roji* that symbolizes leaving behind the dust and troubles of the world. When you live out of your imagination, you leave behind the past and move into new, uncharted areas of success and significance. When people around you make mistakes, learn to affirm their worth and potential and separate their current behavior from their future possibilities.

"WHAT GOT YOU HERE WON'T GET YOU THERE" (GOLDSMITH)

I constantly use the saying, "You cannot meet new challenges with old ways of thinking." To go beyond, to reach new arenas of success that you have never experienced before, you must simply think and act in ways that you have never thought or acted before. You must break with the past and use your imagination to create a new and better world for you and those you associate with. New success in any area of your life will require a break with the old patterns and behaviors that have placed you where you are.

I have been fortunate to coach a women's basketball team that has consistently won twenty-plus games a year. That was a good thing, but we finally reached a point when that did not satisfy any more. We wanted to grow and expand and do more. I knew what level of work had helped us reach our past successes and the work and thinking it took to get there. To reach a new level of success, I knew we would have to act and think in different ways than the past. This started with me, as the saying goes, "To change the world, you must change yourself."

You can use this mode of thinking to create new results in your personal and professional lives. You know better than anyone what has gotten you to where you currently are, if you will confront the brutal facts. This may require you to step back from your patterns and decision making and truly examine the underlying causes of your own behavior and the behavior of your group. You now have a choice to make if you would like to continue to reach those results or create new results, and this will require expanded thinking. I constantly challenge everyone in our organization to go beyond the past and to develop new actions because we understand, "What got us here won't get us there." Sometimes our own success holds us back from our future potential.

If we have been successful in the past, we only figured out what worked up until that day. It does not mean it will be successful today or in the future. It is the past. To move into new arenas of success, we have to make fundamental shifts in our thinking by evaluating what we did in the past and by changing or upgrading our actions. In *Decision No. 1: Experience an Awakening,* I asked you to take a life inventory to see where you currently are. If you were honest about all aspects of your life, it would be easy to diagnose why you are where you are. If you don't like where you are or the level of success you have achieved, then you must change that picture by using your imagination and creating a new picture and acting from that new picture. You must think in new ways and act on those new thoughts.

An unwillingness to break with the old will never create the new. You can be as stubborn as you want to, but just expect to continually hit your head on the same ceiling that you have every year with the same results. A breakthrough may come as a result of a breakdown or through your finally realizing that you will no longer accept the results of the past. Make a conscious decision today that you will spend some time doing nothing but thinking about how you ended up where you are today and how you can move beyond past limitations that quite possibly you created.

THE POWER OF INTENTION: WE CREATE WHAT WE WRITE DOWN

The power of intention is strong, because from intention flows action. As we begin to understand how to move through the Belief and Action Model (Figure 1.1), we understand the process of believing, seeing, doing, and reflecting. The entire process begins with a basic belief in yourself and from there moves into the arena of creating a vision. From that vision there must be self-discipline to act. This self-discipline is built by winning the private internal battles of your life and garnering the capacity to meet the challenges of the world. This juncture is where most people fail. When your intention is strong enough, you will act with unwavering resolve toward your destination, and if you are leading others, you will be fanatically driven in the direction of the group's dreams.

After completing your objectives, it is important to complete the model by reflecting on what you learned and how you can apply the contents to your continuous success. Many people succeed and fail and never take the time to reflect on how it all happened, effectively setting themselves up for similar success or failure over and over again.

The model for success is a continuous circular cycle; this process never ends. It is in constant pursuit of reaching and optimizing your potential, your kinetic energy, which is stored until you utilize it. If you know anything about potential, you know there is absolutely no way to measure it. Potential is an idea, a concept of embryonic growth that you will grow and get better every day from the time you are born until the time you die. The circle of improvement never ends, because you end when it ends. Obviously, along the way you can choose not to grow and learn, but that is simply your choice and will result in stagnation and atrophy. The natural consequence of making this choice is that you will become obsolete in the world and will not be rewarded by your actions.

As we match up our internal dialogue with our external actions we begin to create a synergy between our thoughts and actions that results in progress, as long as those internal thoughts are positive. Studies show that we must stay in a continual growth state, with progress naturally motivating and driving us in our pursuit. This growth state is vital to overcoming a common myth known as "arrival fallacy," the idea that we will be happy when we arrive somewhere in the future. Growth and progression toward a goal, however, keep us engaged in our lives.

We create everything in our life first with our thoughts (intentions) and then by manifesting those thoughts into actions. When we do not believe in ourselves (doubt), we act from that intention and illuminate insecurity and scarcity. We attract more into our lives of what we project, therefore attracting minimal amounts of success because we act according to a paradigm of fear and scarcity. Also, we attract what we put out, so examine the people you are attracting into your life and see if it is because of the intentions you are projecting.

When we have strong thoughts of success and significance, we act from those thoughts and attract high energy back into our lives in the form of success and happiness. If you don't believe me, consider this one concept. Light is positive energy and is much stronger than darkness. If a room is unlit and you turn the lights on, the positive energy overcomes the negative or low energy and the light overcomes the darkness. Equate this to light being positive and darkness being negative or low energy. Energy cannot be created; it can only be transferred. What you will find in your life is that when you match positive internal thoughts with external actions you will attract more positive people and things into your life.

The light in you will serve to illuminate the good in others, and they likewise will reflect that light back to you. This will produce open avenues of communication, respect, and mutual admiration between you and others because you CHOOSE to see the good in them and likewise bring out the best in them to see in you. This will lubricate the process of communication with everyone you deal with, making your life more integrated and complete. At the same time, there are low-energy people out there simply acting from their negative thoughts. Be a light to those people, not a judge. Be a model, not a critic. Your light will overcome their darkness and low energy. All you can control is your response to their stimulus, and in good time the very response you cultivate could actually control the stimulus they offer you.

You will find that these types of low-energy people will simply not want to associate with you and will choose to find other low-energy people and massage each other's hearts while they complain about their lot in life. When you see these people, you can choose either to work to illuminate the good in them or disassociate from them. Either way, don't forget that you hold the keys to unlock either positive or negative energy. No other person can take this good energy away from you unless you allow them to.

INSPIRATIONAL THINGS HAPPEN IN INSPIRATIONAL SETTINGS: BUILD PLACES IN YOUR LIFE TO THINK

Inspiration happens in inspirational places and around inspirational people. As I have stated throughout the book and if you have read either of my other books, I write while I vacation in inspirational settings. My first two books were written on Florida beaches, and much of the content of this book was developed while cruising to Alaska or in cabins in the woods across the country. I have been inspired the entire time. The word *inspire* means to "breathe life into." There is just something spiritual that connects to the good and spiritual side of you when you are in nature. Nature flows naturally and with ease. Your life should be the same way, flowing with ease. This doesn't mean there won't be any obstacles. By viewing adversity as a means to improve the quality of your life, you change the picture of bad things happening to you into good things happening to you. Many times we force situations in life when they could just naturally occur if we chose to quit resisting.

Deepak Chopra (1994) postulated that everything is exactly the way it should be at this moment in your life and discussed the law of least resistance in his book *Seven Spiritual Laws of Success*. If you accept things as they are and remove judgment, you begin to be fully present in the moment. This in essence will free up energy to enjoy the here and now versus worry about the past or stress over the future. This also refers to unintentional manifestations where things happen in your life because you are simply aligned with your source. You may call this luck, but the fact remains that luck favors those who are prepared and who perform consistently. They work from intentional manifestation, and because they work from this intention, good things happen to them.

To unleash the creativity of your imagination I suggest that you go somewhere that inspires creativity. A park, near water, your backyard, a reading room, the library, around smart people, wherever could inspire YOU to be creative. I regularly meet with creative people to stir ideas and emotions inside me that awaken the creative side I need to be innovative. Everyone's life becomes stagnant and needs to be awakened, and usually this comes with seeing something inspirational or by being around inspired people. Reading is another common avenue to inspiration and opens the imagination to see things multidimensionally rather then myopically. The important thing is that you regularly include creativity sessions in your life based on your particular lifestyle. This will enrich the process of learning and growing and will make the journey more fun and exciting.

Not long ago I built a house around the idea of inspiration so that I would no longer have to travel to inspiring places to feel this inspiration. Instead, I could immerse myself in it. I became intentional about building my own sources of inspiration with water, serenity, peace of mind, and happiness. When I began to understand that we need to be just as intentional about our personal happiness as we are about our work goals, I began to see that we need goals and aspirations in all areas of our lives. I encourage you to create a place where you can visit (perhaps your home) daily and drink deeply from inspiration. Stopping to create a mind-set of gratitude for what we have in life and appreciating the work and sacrifice to manifest those things will give you a good perspective that will bring more into your life.

DREAMING THROUGH VISION AND DISCIPLINE: TAKE THOUGHT AND TURN IT INTO REALITY

Once you have found your voice in life and have some clear direction from practicing *Decision No. 1: Experience an Awakening,* you are on your way to expressing that voice to others in several ways. Remember, this voice is when you are marrying your natural, God-given talent and passions with a need in the world and operating from the sweet spot of your life. You are trading your talents and passions for purpose rather than merely trading your time and energy for money. The first two ways toward expression are through the creation of a vision for your life. This vision is seeing the world through your mind's eye, allowing you to create a new and exciting path to a better world. Once you have created this vision, your life has a context for the journey, and everyone loves a journey.

To reach any destination you must cultivate the discipline to act in the moments of choice to reach that vision. This is where emotional push-ups come into play in your life and where many people falter. As I suggested earlier, having a life of fulfillment and happiness around passionate execution and significant contribution all flows back to taking full responsibility for your life and your actions or any lack thereof. Between your stimulus and response will be a space, and in that space lies your ability to choose. It is from here that self-discipline is built. The word *discipline* comes from the term *disciple,* which means to give yourself to a person or cause you believe in. You can effectively become a disciple to yourself and win the private battles necessary in order to win the public ones. You own your future. You're the only person who can see it.

You are the only person who knows what intellectual capital you have in your head that you need to manifest. If you do not cultivate this vision or the discipline to act on the vision you will simply remain where you are, and time will continue to pass you by. We get roughly twenty-five thousand mornings in our lifetime, and you are either making each day your masterpiece or settling into a life of mediocrity. Settling means to gradually decline into an average place. If you want a remarkable life, you must learn to marry and bridge vision and action together. All great dreamers are not necessarily achievers, but all great achievers tend to be dreamers.

You cultivate a vision by dreaming, by thinking big, by expanding, and by breaking with old, antiquated thought patterns into new ways of living your life. Each year in my organization I create a theme. Many years ago the theme was "Good to Great," from the popular Jim Collins book. I encouraged my constituents to decide what *great* looked like. They came up with five things. That was the vision. Everything we did worked backward from that vision. It was a powerful theme, because it offered us a mission and a purpose that we could work toward. Another theme was "The Power of Intention," based on the work of Dr. Wayne Dyer. I teach from his conclusions and help our people believe that they are worthy of fulfilling their dreams. For me to convince them that they are worthy, I must first believe it is a worthy mission and we can fulfill it. From belief stems vision, and then you must have the discipline and the execution to complete the vision through repetitive, consistent actions. This will build confidence around the memory of success. Begin today by building a vision of where you are going in your life and start toward that vision by completing and executing the small victories needed to win the ultimate victory.

Life is a series of small successes that build up until one day you are a big success. Once you reach a stable level of success (find your voice), you can then begin to search for significance (helping others find their voices). In essence, life is about detecting your gifts and then giving those gifts away to as many people as you can.

MARRYING PASSION AND CONSCIENCE
WHILE EXECUTING THE DREAM

I have not talked much about something I feel adamant about when it comes to living a life of significant contribution, namely, passion. This is the fuel that drives your car, gets you excited, rows your boat, and helps you to dig down deep to find meaning amid the chaos in your life. Passion is defined as an irresistible belief for motive or action. Without passion, life is dull and mundane. With it, life is exciting and adventurous. As I travel the country I have discovered that so many people lack passion. Because of this lack of love from the heart (passion), they plod through jobs, relationships, friendships, and any endeavor they undertake. To be great at anything, I firmly believe you must have passion for it.

I started writing books and speaking because I had a deep desire to help others fulfill their potential in life by encouraging them to act. This passion started in coaching but then manifested as speaking, consulting, and writing. When I traveled the world, I began to see what I said lit the inner fire among people everywhere and I could see their eyes shine. This affirmation only fueled my passion for exploring the field of personal growth and organizational effectiveness, because I knew that the only way to grow an organization was to grow the people. In the process I understood that you simply could not have one without the other. I also knew the tremendous amount of personal growth that I had experienced through educating my mind and heart and the benefits my organization had garnered because of it. From that I knew I *had* to share my gift with others.

I hope my passion for continual growth is contagious and has rubbed off on you. It is something that is difficult to give to others but something that you must seek to give away. If you want the people you associate with to be passionate about anything, you must first model the behavior you want from them. Remember, be a light of passionate behavior, not a critic. Be a model, not a judge. Throw light on others, and maybe in the process they will begin to feel the spirit move within them. The word *inspiration* comes from "spirit within," and the word *enthusiasm* derives from "God within." Help others feel the spirit and God within them.

When thinking about what you specifically need to do with your life (find your voice), ask this question, "What is it that I cannot not do?" Replace the question with, "What do I need to do with the previous question?" and you will get closer to finding your voice.

Conscience is that internal voice that longs to connect to something larger; it is a need to leave a legacy and live a life of deep meaning and significant contribution. In order to do this, you must begin the exploration process of finding your voice so you can inspire others to find theirs. Once we find our voices in our vocations and understand that most of the good that is done in the world is in and through organizations, we begin to place our time, talents, and energy in organizations that we believe in and behind the causes we deem worthy.

One person, however, can make a significant difference in the world by continually growing his or her influence and deeply impacting others. Through emotional identification, what we have to say can strongly resonate with others in such a way that it truly transforms lives. Many of you have been transformed by something you read or saw on television. This emotional identification is so strong it actually feels like you know the people who are influencing you. It is important that we continually expand and educate our conscience and develop the capacity to listen to it in tough moments of choice. This will be our guide to wisdom and clarity and help us stay out of personal and professional tough spots.

Try for just one day to listen to your conscience and connect the dots of what it is trying to urge you to do. Develop the internal discipline to act on that conscience and see how much better you feel about the results. We're not always looking for peace of mind but rather peace of conscience, because we have married our passion with our internal voice of right and wrong so we can lay our heads down at the end of the day and know we did all we could to win. When we don't have these four things—vision, discipline, passion, and conscience—we wander without direction and purpose through life and become totally reactive to the world. Jim Rohn said, "Either you run the day or the day runs you."

Marry these four things with the ability to break with the past in an effort to expand your dream maker, and you'll start to create a bigger future that is much better than your past. Make a fundamental decision that your best days are never in your past, but always in your future.

Chapter 3 Summary: Seven Action Items to Design Your Own Dream

1. *Today,* I will live out of my imagination instead of my memory. I will consciously spend thirty minutes reflecting on my life in the four areas of body, mind, heart, and spirit, and I will focus on improving my skills, knowledge, desire, and beliefs. Today I will plan a trip to a place that resonates with me so my mind and heart are awakened to the beauty of life. Today, I will spend time reflecting and focusing on my dreams.

2. *Today,* I will forgive myself for my past transgressions. I will realize that all people have made poor decisions, and I will allow those past decisions to serve as a light of positive energy to my future. I will forgive those who have transgressed against me and hurt me and lose the burden of revenge in my heart. I will not be ashamed of my past decisions or wallow in regret, because I fully understand that only when I use those decisions for future improvement are they beneficial to me and others. I will start today off with a fresh slate and allow others the opportunity to start fresh with me. I will understand that life is much too short to allow my past (in any area of my life) to hold my future hostage.

3. *Today,* I will fully understand that I cannot meet new challenges or reach new successes with old, outdated ways of thinking. I will think and act in new ways and empower myself to think big and act on those thoughts. Through an active inventory of my life I will investigate what rendered past results and work to create new results based on new knowledge and new concepts. Today, I will spend time sharing and garnering new information that will make me a valuable commodity in the workplace. I will focus on solu-

tions versus problems. Today, I will think in ways I've never thought before and see life in ways I've never seen before. I will become the light to others that illuminates and radiates constant and continual growth.

4. *Today*, I will understand that actions come from intentions. I will examine my thoughts and my internal dialogue to match positive thoughts with positive actions. I will work diligently to create congruence with my mission and my moments of life. I will work from an intention to manifest positive thoughts while all the time knowing that good things will happen to me if I move confidently in the direction of my dreams. Today, I will intend to make a difference in the lives of others and will fully understand my role as an important part of the whole.

5. *Today*, I will unleash the creative process by spending some time reflecting. I will go to a place where I can stop and think and connect to my source of inspiration. I will understand that inspiration happens in inspirational settings and around inspirational people. I will model inspiration around those I associate with, fully understanding that I have a choice between stimulus and response and choosing how I respond to the many stimuli I face daily. Today, I will visit with others who inspire and uplift me and choose to disassociate from those who project negative draining energy.

6. *Today*, I will express my voice through vision and discipline. I will consciously examine where I am going with my life and will see the world through my mind's eye. I will walk my talk and begin to build the self-discipline and capacity to act in the daily moments of life. I will fully realize that to reach a destination, it must first be designed, and I will align both my thoughts and actions so I can reach that destination. Today, I will move with purpose and inten-

tion toward my dreams, and I will act on three high-value activities (action items that yield optimum results) toward that destination.

7. *Today,* I will act with passion and conscience to express my voice. Today, I will move with fire and intent and will live inspired. Today, I will work with a fervor and drive uncommon to ordinary people, and I will be driven by my conscience as well as by my sense of meaning and purpose in life. Today, I will reflect on my vocation and truly see if it intersects with my passion and conscience. Today, I will practice compassion for others and fully understand that I have the power to be a tremendous creative force in the world. Today, I will live life to the fullest without negativity, jealously, scarcity, or anger.

Chapter 4

Learn to Play Up

IF YOU WANT TO GET BETTER IN LIFE, LEARN TO PLAY WITH PEOPLE BETTER THAN YOU

As I BEGIN THIS chapter, I want to share a story from my life to illustrate the concept of learning to play up. Recently I made a conscious decision to rid myself of the worry of what others think about me. When I first started chasing my dreams of impacting people around the country, I was a high school basketball coach. I took the necessary steps with Web sites, books, and a message, and I went out and began to speak to anybody who would listen. My message got better, and the audiences gave positive feedback. I knew this was my calling. What I found out was that many of my professional colleagues secretly made fun of me behind my back for speaking and writing. They supported me to my face but undermined me when I wasn't around. I've always heard it said that we try to make others look small so we can make ourselves look big. I'm not sure if that was the case here or not, but what I did realize was "So what?"

Our society is set up from an early age not to be supportive of others when they chase their dreams, as if our whole lives are determined by competition. When you learn to play up in your life, you become less worried about the gossip or undercurrent of resistance you'll sense from those closest to you and become more concerned about how your dream will impact many others who will appreciate what you have to offer. The only way to stop the negative voices in the background is show with your actions that you're the real deal, not with words but with results. There will still be a long line of people who take offense to your success, but don't worry about them. They're just trying to find their place in the world and most likely could benefit from what you have to say if they would just stop and listen.

Stop and reflect for a moment on your own life and how you have allowed others to define you and criticize you in ways that have shaped your decisions and defined your own self-worth. Unfortunately we live in a society that promotes pushing others down to get where we're going. Deep within each of us is a need to be loved and accepted, but we must first love and accept ourselves internally before we can return that love back to others, even to those who transgress against us.

Have you ever been in a room or with others who claim to be your friends only to feel the judging, the comparing, the jealously, or the contentious spirit they bring to the conversation? Just yesterday I was with a group of people where this spirit of downgrading, demeaning, and competition dominated the air. I discussed this concept with another person, and he said to me that there were basically two groups of people—acquaintances and friends—and he could count on one hand his true friends. I refuted that concept and shared with him that I thought there were three levels of interaction with others: acquaintances, friends, and advocates. Acquaintances are people you speak to, know little about, but could become friends. Friends are people who you have shared experiences with—either positive or negative—and could be called upon to help in a situation, if it was possible for them. But advocates are people with whom you have shared a lot and who would never judge you or criticize you for your actions. Advocates will always support you, especially in your absence. Stephen Covey eloquently said, "If you want to retain those who are present, be loyal to those who are absent." We simply lose trust and credibility with everyone when we judge and criticize.

That experience awakened something inside me and helped me to see that we should never allow others to define us, because they will in nonthreatening ways to them. More important, we should rid ourselves of the worry associated with just friends. More important than that concept is that we never become the kind of people who judge, criticize, ridicule, compare, compete, contend, or seek to belittle. We have two choices in life: one is to take the road to mediocrity (which is the road most traveled), and the other is to take the road to greatness and meaning. The beauty of life is that you get to choose which road you take. Just make sure you choose wisely. Decide today to cleanse your life of the toxins that will never help you get where you truly deserve to go. Be more concerned about building stark raving, crazy advocates than just friends.

My first piece of advice here is to create a Target 25 list of advocates: those who know you, love you, and support your dreams. Water this Target 25 list with a minimum of four face-to-face meetings per person, without limits, per year. Send them two gifts each year. Hold a luncheon in their honor once a year so they can share with each other. And ALWAYS be there when they call. These people are your biggest advocates. The secret to strengthening your advocates is to advocate for them. When you learn to play up, you don't have time for pettiness in life. Focus not on who you used to be, but on who you can become with the right people around you.

Never Devalue Your Self-Worth and Potential

You are on this earth for a specific reason. You are valuable and have the same needs everyone else has, which is to:

Live: The body's need
Love: The heart's need
Learn: The mind's need
Leave a Legacy: The spirit's need

As you begin to tap into your birth gifts, you realize that you gain internal value when you live your life in service to others in a meaningful way that is tied to your passion and talents. So many people I meet have devalued themselves because of what others have said to them (environment), what has happened to them (psychological), or some past failure they have allowed to hold their future hostage. You should never ever treat yourself as second class, because the moment you do, you encourage others to do the exact same thing. In ALL interactions, people should get the best version of you, not some phony representative that only comes out when you're in the mood. Many times, confidence is the deciding factor that separates one success story from a failure. Confidence can be defined as the memory of success, and you garner success through belief, vision, action, and reflection (the Manifestation Model).

I fully realize that many of us live on our reflection from the social mirror (allowing others' opinions of us to dictate how we feel about ourselves), but confidence can be entirely internal, and it flows from the memory of success. We garner success through consistent repetition. When we allow others to define us based on their opinions of us or their actions toward us, we disempower ourselves and empower their weakness to control us. When we live our life around values and self-evident principles, these can become our lighthouses and can offer our internal spring of confidence to work toward our dreams.

To truly reach an inner peace, you must clearly define the values by which you want to live, work in the directions of your dreams with a passion, and don't ever devalue what you are doing. All those people who may laugh at you on the front end will be converted to believers on the back end. Remember, talk is cheap, but action will make believers out of disbelievers. Use negative external factors to fuel your dreams and accelerate your progress. I've found that by using negativity as the intellectual firepower to achieve greatness that it can become a strong motivator for almost anyone. *Learn to Play Up* here by building a "Dream Team" around you who believes in you and the vision you want to create, not people who constantly judge and criticize you or make fun of your dreams.

INTERNAL THOUGHTS BECOME EXTERNAL THINGS

What are you telling yourself right now? I'm not good enough? I'm not smart enough? I'm not good-looking enough? I'm not thin enough? These are all reactive responses to the social mirror of society. For us to change what we feel on the outside, we have to train ourselves to clean up our internal language so that it accurately reflects a confidence in ourselves that can drive our actions. Low self-esteem stems from a lack of belief in oneself, which flows from our internal dialogue. When we change the internal picture, we know that we do have something unique to offer, and we can constantly grow in the areas of our deficiencies and build confidence through repetition.

This internal emotional strength is similar to building physical strength. How do you build physical strength? You lift weights consistently, you run consistently, you exercise consistently. You build emotional strength exactly the same way, through consistent deposits into your emotional bank account. You win the private battles of your soul by making and keeping commitments to yourself and to others. You hold yourself accountable, you build integrity, and you translate your mission daily in the tough moments of choice. You educate and obey your conscience by living a principle-centered life.

One of the strongest ways to find yourself and build your internal dialogue is to immerse yourself in service to others. As you illuminate the good in others, you will light your own fire, recognize the value you have to offer, and reaffirm the worth and potential in yourself. Remember, one definition of leadership is communicating and validating the worth and potential in others so clearly that they begin to see it in themselves.

When you are learning how to play up, you must begin to surround yourself with others who affirm and validate your worth and potential. Many times we criticize others for weaknesses that we possess. We judge others based on their actions and judge ourselves based on our intentions. Your internal dialogue has been hardwired with deep scripting from an early age from a number of areas, and software has been installed into you by who you associate with. To grow your internal dialogue, I suggest reading and listening to positive information on how to overcome negative thoughts and emotions that shackle your potential versus releasing it. Remember this, internal dialogue or thoughts become external things. Thoughts become things if you think on them long enough.

Dennis Waitley observed that when you're going through a rough spot in life, look back at the many successes you've experienced, and you will know you can win. The ability to process failure and adversity is vital to happiness and sustainability. We'll tackle how to use adversity for good in chapter 5 (Add Value Versus Subtract It).

Belief: Where Do You Get It and How Can You Find It?

Everything begins with belief. Even before you can see anything in your life, you must first believe that a better world can exist. Vision tied to discipline tied to action is followed by reflection (refer to the Belief and Action model 1). Notice that I said that belief must be in self first and in the cause second. Every humanistic organizational problem begins at the personal level and stems from dysfunctionality with self. If you do not believe in yourself and have not developed your voice, it will be very difficult to lend your voice to a cause you deem worthy. If you have found your voice and have found a cause you believe in, then you are well on your way to contributing your unique voice to a cause you deem worthy.

At the intersection of talent, passion, needs of the world, and conscience lies most likely your vocation in life. When we go to work in jobs and do not believe in ourselves, we neglect our mind, heart, and spirit and treat ourselves as second-class. This usually results in giving others permission to treat us as second-class. They can see that we have not paid the emotional price for security and confidence and that we do not value ourselves. This red light will get you passed over every time as you try to move up the food chain. It will lead to discontent in both yourself and in your job.

The second part of this equation is belief or lack thereof in the causes you choose to spend your time in. Much of the legacy you will leave in your life will be in and through the organizations in which you choose to participate. If you believe fully in a cause and the vision of that cause, then you will most likely engage all dimensions (body, mind, heart, and spirit) to that cause. You will give of your whole self.

This is really what we are trying so desperately to do in the knowledge worker era. Our goal is to unleash the latent and undeveloped potential in all our people. In essence, help them find their voices in life. When you do not believe in the cause you work for, both your heart and your spirit will be neglected because the cause's principles go against your conscience. This lack of congruence will produce feelings of discontent, and you will be unhappy and unfulfilled with the cause. If you have ever heard anyone refer to having a broken spirit or lost passion in their job, it's a manifestation of neglecting their heart and the spirit.

Similar feelings persist in your personal life if you associate with people who live by different principles than you. You can either change what you value (reactive) or have the emotional strength to stand up for what you believe in (proactive). You must do this with balance of both courage and consideration for the other person, and this normally defines your personal maturity level. In my book *The Inspirational Leader* I noted that people want to wake up in the morning and go to a job they love, work for a cause they deem worthy, and labor for a leader in whom they believe. When you find that synergistic mix, you will be in an environment that optimizes and unleashes the human potential inside you. If you are not currently in that position, you probably stay in a funk, do not believe in the mission or leader of the organization, and get all of your satisfaction off the job.

The challenge with this way of thinking is that the largest percentage of your life will be spent working. Remember that the needs of people are based on a holistic approach to living (body—to live, mind—to learn, heart—to love, spirit—to leave a legacy). Finding your voice in life and in your vocation will lead to significant contribution and passionate execution around what matters most to you.

Here's some simple advice. If you don't believe in the cause you're associating with, such as your job, then find another bus to get on in life. Life is much too short to go to a job you don't believe in or work for a leader you don't support. This isn't the hokeypokey where you can just put part of yourself in and leave the best parts out. People go to work every day and leave their most important parts at home: their heart and their mind. They quit, but they forgot to tell other people. When you understand the holistic approach I speak to (body, mind, heart, and spirit), you understand that you simply have a choice about how much you offer to the cause.

LOSE THE EMOTIONAL CANCERS IN YOUR LIFE

I do not know any other way to say this: Lose the negativity in your life. This means the negative internal thoughts, the negative people around you, the negative things you tolerate, the reactiveness from both you and the people around you, all of it. Always remember: We encourage what we allow. To live a life of happiness you must build the emotional strength to take full responsibility for your life and decide what you will tolerate and what you will not.

As you build that emotional strength, you will build an immune system to negative people and circumstances. In fact we attract back into our life what we put out, so if you are positive and proactive, you will most likely attract positive and proactive people into your life. Negative people will see your positive behavior as kryptonite and run in the other direction. Your stimulus will create the very response you are looking for. Have you ever tried to be mad at someone who will not be mad back? Have you ever tried to stay upset with someone who just moves on? Have you ever tried to argue with someone who will not argue back? Frustrating, huh? You be the light that illuminates the good in others.

The hardest thing you will ever have to do is see the good in people and radiate and affirm that good. The easy thing to do is to compare, criticize, complain, contend, and compete for self-worth and potential through bad-mouthing, undermining, trash talking, or continually demeaning another's spirit. Listen and feel for the heart and soul of others as they communicate to you. The psychological air and space you give them will affirm and validate their worth and potential in clear ways that will illuminate the positive and hide the negative.

For some reason, many of us allow negative people to drain the very positive energy we have. This is a reactive response to the world and disempowers us and gives our power to their weaknesses. There is certainly enough negativity in the world, and you can be drawn into it if you choose to, but successful people are not negative people. The best people understand that they are borrowing strength from a formal position when they use their position of power in negative ways to get things done. This is based on a paradigm of fear and insecurity. This will build weakness in the relationship in two ways: in self (because you used your formal power to coerce someone into action) and in others (because you bullied them into action).

Moral authority, where people openly choose to follow you, is a much better avenue from which to act. This area to refine is simple. Decide today that you will not allow the moods or feelings of others to steal away your internal strength and confidence. Practice being a light—not a judge, a model, or a critic.

When I coached high school basketball, many of the young ladies on my team would say, "Coach Burt, I just can't wait to get out of high school because there is just so much drama in high school, and when I get out it will be so much better." I would look at them and say, "Girl, when you get out of high school it will be three times worse. Adults are worse at drama than kids are."

Drama is something that never goes away. You either make a conscious choice to participate in it or you don't. If you want a peaceful life full of joy and happiness, then you simply don't have time to participate in the endless drama that is served up every day around the world.

PLAYING UP BEGINS BY "SHARPENING YOUR OWN SAW"

The key to unlimited opportunity is through education. In *The Richest Man in Babylon* (Clason, 2004), George Clason says, "Education is the key to our success. Every action we take is driven by our thoughts and our thoughts are no wiser than our understandings." The question then becomes how do we expand our understandings? From my thought process, this comes from two places: education and experiences. Knowledge, if used properly, can truly become influential. in When I refer to educating yourself, I don't necessarily mean that you have to go back to college. That option simply is not available for everyone, but young people who have the opportunity should think about the fact that the average college graduate will make over $600,000 in his or lifetime more than over a person who does not attend college.

If college or continuing a formal education is not an option for you, then the key is to want to grow in your particular field and to grow your knowledge base. This adds tremendous value to your life and the organization's life and makes you a hot commodity. As you constantly learn new trends in your field, your mind will be challenged, you will be inspired, and you will begin to share your knowledge with others. This also helps in your pursuit of being the best at what you do. Remember, the mind's need is to learn constantly and grow, and this can only be done by challenging current boundaries.

My own learning did not accelerate until I was twenty-five years old, and from that point forward I wanted to read everything I could get my hands on. I became a sponge for learning and growth. My friends and family could not understand why I constantly wanted to learn. I simply told them I was deeply passionate about personal growth, being the best in my field, and sharing my newfound knowledge with others. The best investment I ever made was pursuing both my master's and doctoral degrees. Both of those experiences were transformational and lit my fire of learning and growing. There are many ways to learn in this information era: online education, seminars, the exchange of knowledge and ideas with your cohorts, the Internet, mentoring, educational television, and reading. Just by picking up this book and reading this far, you have made an internal choice to improve yourself.

I shared earlier with you that the mind is elastic and grows when it is challenged. You must begin the process of challenging your mind. How can you do this? It is simple. You can read, listen to educational CDs, attend seminars, speak to the best people in your field, share your knowledge with others, and do anything that challenges you to think. If you are truly in your passion area for your vocation, you will not have to be pushed to want to learn.

Thomas Friedman (2006) in *The World Is Flat* said, "Nobody works harder at learning than a curious kid." If you want to continue learning, you have to become curious about something. I hope it is your field or vocational area. Friedman also has a formula for success: $CQ + PQ > IQ$. CQ stands for Curious Quotient, PQ for Passion Quotient, and IQ for Intellect Quotient. He believes that a passionate person who is curious is a much better hire any day than a purely intellectual person. I agree. I would take a person who is curious and has built high levels of emotional intelligence and who has passion any day in the workplace.

Not seeking to learn will breed complacency, and complacency will never place you among the elite in your category. You must intend to be the best and work backward from there. To do that, becoming a continual learner is simply part of the process. Also, as you learn more, you will begin to transcend one market, and your skills will make you accessible for more jobs, and that will open you up to a better financial life.

When you do not learn, you choose to pigeonhole yourself into one profession and lock the door on what could be a self-imposed prison for many years. Remember, the average person will spend 45 percent of his or her life working. That is a long time to get up and go to a job you do not love and your heart is not into. When you don't educate yourself, you could be locking yourself into that job for a long time. The new era is built around knowledge workers who constantly grow and learn. Get in on this trend or be left out of future opportunity. It's pretty much that simple.

CHANGE THE PICTURE OR CHANGE THE SITUATION

If I were to ask you what your profession is, what would you tell me? Whenever I ask that question in front of a group I almost always get the same responses: I'm a nurse, a supervisor, a manager, a crew leader, a factory worker, etc. Then I ask them what they really do for a living. They become frustrated.

When I asked that question of a nurse at one of my lectures, she finally said, "Look, I help people when they are sick, okay?"

I pressed, "Do you save people's lives?"

She said, "Yes."

I said, "Do you help people at their most uncomfortable times in life?"

She said, "Yes."

"Well, then," I said, "you have got a whole lot bigger reason for waking up in the morning than to just be a nurse or to pick up a paycheck."

What is it that you really do for a living? Speaking for myself, I could give you the standard answer that I'm a coach, a speaker, an author, an athletic director, and a consultant. And that would be very generic. But what I really wake up in the morning to do is to spotlight the potential in others, speak to people to create enthusiasm and action toward significance, write books to inspire others to become their best, lead people toward a vision in an athletic department, and enable greatness in organizations across the country. Those are bigger reasons to get up and go to work in the morning, and they are integrated into my whole life. They permeate my existence and give me meaning and purpose. This lifestyle is not compartmentalized but rather integrated around what I love doing.

My challenge to you today is to change the picture of what you do for a living and to see your profession as not only a means to a financial end but also a journey of self-discovery and service to others. If you do not believe in the cause you go to work for every day or the people you do it with, then find another cause. Remember, *Decision No. 1: Experience an Awakening* unlocks the door to taking responsibility for your life, and that includes the vocation you choose to participate in.

Many of you likely got into your profession because you loved a certain aspect of it in the beginning. You had passion and enthusiasm. You must always reconnect to that passion, especially if you believe you have lost it. Find a big reason to wake up and go to it every morning, and you'll begin to see your life as being integrated around what you love. This will add fulfillment to your life as well as a much-needed meaning and purpose. The key is to search and work to make the transition from effectiveness to greatness daily. As Stephen Covey noted, we all take one of two paths in life: one is the broad, well-traveled road to mediocrity, the other is the road to greatness and meaning. Which road will you choose today?

In the grand scheme of things you've got two options about how you see what you see. You can change the picture or you can change the situation. Choose wisely.

THE BOOK COVER HELPS OTHERS WANT TO OPEN THE BOOK

Ninety-three percent of all communication is nonverbal. Every time we walk into a room, sit in a chair, sit in a meeting, look at another, or just be, we are communicating with others. Can you tell what others have on their minds when they do not say a word? Can you tell when there are ulterior motives and hidden agendas based on the actions of others? If you want to live a life of deep meaning and significant contribution, you have to learn to project success on your personal movie screen.

Some of you could be wondering why what you project to others has to do with your own professional success. As we move up the continuum and begin to practice *Decision No. 6: Build Up Versus Tear Down*, we see that the only way to significance is through others. To do this we have to project positive vibes. Those vibes will always come back to us through the aforementioned power of intention. I speak to all types of people, and there are certain universal principles that always apply. Smiling will almost always result in a smile back. Please and thank you will always make the person who offered the service feel better, and a healthy positive attitude will always go further than a negative one.

In the workplace, movers and shakers rarely have time for negative attitudes or projections of people who are not on board. Leaders are looking for individuals who realize that life is not always easy and the best way to predict the future is to create it. Once you have climbed the ladder of success, as many of you will, don't ever forget that now you have more influence and can do more good than you previously could. Never underestimate the power of positive projections. There's nothing that can turn someone who's a big fan off quicker than a negative attitude. Start today by becoming aware of what you're projecting on your movie screen. Change the picture if it's negative.

I know many people who have developed a functional blindness to their own defect of projecting negativity. When others let you in on the secret that you have a bad attitude, take heed to their advice. What we project to others with how we dress, how we speak, how we interact, and how we respond lets them know if there is a gentle and caring soul on the inside. Some statistics suggest that we have thirty seconds to make a positive first impression by our outside cover. If we mess up this first interaction, it will take twenty-one positive interactions to overcome that first negative one. With Web sites, they tell us it takes only seven seconds to form an opinion. Be real clear about what you are projecting to others. You don't have to wear a three-thousand-dollar suit everywhere, but you should always look presentable and smile, because it costs nothing to generate positive energy. You'll get back what you put out, trust me.

Chapter 4 Summary: Seven Action Items
to Manifest the Key Clean Up

1. *Today,* I will value my self-worth. I will not allow anyone's judg-

ments, criticisms, or negative thinking to limit my future potential. Today, I will accept the fact that I have made mistakes and transgressed against others. I will live today with happiness in my heart, and I will accept others and myself as we are. I will treat myself first-class in all things I do, and I will begin every endeavor with a belief in myself and in the cause I am engaged. Today, I will play up with people better than I, and I will not allow my own insecurities to stop me from associating and learning from those who are better than I.

2. *Today,* I will change my internal dialogue to one that values and appreciates my uniqueness. I will understand that I am special, I have many talents to offer, and I will constantly affirm my own worth and potential. I will pay the price to build emotional security so I can decide what my own worth is, rather than accept how others define me.

3. *Today,* I will begin everything I do with a belief in self and cause. I will have this belief because I fully know that I have built emotional strength through consistent repetition and practice. Today, I will choose to participate only in things that I believe in, and I will choose to disassociate from the causes that are not in alignment with my heart and spirit and in areas from which I am not passionate. I will seek to create a synergy between my talents, passions, needs of the world, and my conscience that will manifest meaning and contribution. Today, if I have lost my voice, I will believe and dream again.

4. *Today,* I will complete a personal inventory and cleanse my life of any present toxins. This may be with a job, a friendship, a relationship, or a cause. No longer will I allow others to define me. Today, I will experience an awakening of life and energy, and I will work

with purpose, passion, presence, and perseverance toward my dreams. Today, I will take out the trash and not look back. I will work to make positive deposits in the emotional bank accounts of others through service and contribution. Today, I will become less interested in making friends and more interested in building stark raving, crazy advocates.

5. *Today,* I will make a choice to fight the emotional cancer of complacency. Today, I will not allow myself to stagnate or fall victim to atrophy. Today, I will make the most important investment I can: an investment in self. Today, I will make a conscious choice to become a constant, continual learner. Today, I will seek opportunities to grow and expand through the sharing of knowledge, meaningful conversations, and reading. Today, I will search for opportunities to attend seminars and learn from the best in the world. Today, I will grow and never return to my previous dimensions.

6. *Today,* I will change the picture about what I do for a living. I will no longer see my job as a means to a financial end. Today, I will seek to serve, contribute, execute, and believe in the mission of the organization. Today, I will awake up with a purpose, a vision, a passion, and an intention to improve the greater good through my talents. Today, I will make a difference in the world and in the lives of those I interact with. Today, I will find my voice in my current job and move toward significance. Today, I will work with a fervor that will radiate purpose in the workplace.

7. *Today,* I will grow my self-awareness to fully realize what I project on my personal movie screen. Today, I will radiate positive energy. I will illuminate the positive in others, and I will allow negative energy to bounce off me. Today, I will fully understand how important my attitude is to success, and I will seek to reward the positive

attitudes of those around me. Today, I will fully understand that leadership is a choice, just as a positive disposition is, and I will seek to communicate and validate the potential in others in clear ways that they can begin to see it in themselves. Today, I will be a light that overtakes the darkness of cynicism and negativity. Today, I will model the behavior I want from others.

Chapter 5

Make Learning a Way of Being

EVERY DAY, IN EVERY WAY, MAKE A DECISION TO LEARN

MANY YEARS AGO I began to use the phrase "becoming humble and teachable" as a way to show how learning begins. This saying originated at my office while I was discussing the six emotional cancers with my players. I was outlining which emotional cancer was the most prevalent in each player's grade level. I happened to have a senior in my office, and I said, "This is simple. You have the knowledge, the skills, and the belief in yourself and the cause. The biggest battle you will fight daily is maintaining a burning desire to compete at the highest levels. The emotional cancer you will face will simply be complacency."

As soon as I shared that statement, the next words came out of my mouth: "You must remain humble and teachable and fully understand that the more knowledge we garner, the more we grow our circle of ignorance. We do this because we come to the realization that there are so many things that we still have to learn."

From that day forward I have used those statements in both my life and the life of my organization. When you stop learning, you stop growing, and if you ever reach a point of arrogance and really believe that you know everything there is to know, you effectively make yourself obsolete in the market.

Many of you reading this book have been in jobs for long periods of time and have allowed yourself to stagnate and become a victim of atrophy. You, too, are facing the emotional cancer of complacency, which I think is one of the biggest emotional cancers in this country.

In this chapter I discuss the key of listening to the all voices around you. I will encourage you first to listen to your conscience, that small, still voice inside you that, if educated properly, will steer you toward congruence and alignment with your spirit and source. I will also encourage you to form your own board of directors, a group of people who can offer wisdom at the crossroads of your life.

I'm convinced that we are moving to an age of wisdom. As Peter Senge (2004) wrote in *Presence,* "As complexity increases, the need for wisdom grows, even as our wisdom atrophies."

Don't fall victim to complacency. Seek and listen to those wise voices around you and make every week an upward spiral of effective living and learning. Part of this chapter will also become about your making a key fundamental decision to continue your learning after your formal education is over. Many people become "past focused" and believe that once they are done with their schooling that they are done learning. If you want a future that is bigger than your present circumstances, then you'll have to pick up a book, go to a seminar, listen to a CD, find a mentor, watch others perform, and have a natural desire to learn and grow. What I would like to see you do is weave learning into the fabric of your everyday life with specific, intentional streams of learning in key components and knowledge areas you need to be ultrasuccessful.

Learning Starts by Listening

The next time you are making a big decision, between your stimulus and response, simply be quiet and listen. Listen to what? Your conscience. Your conscience is the internal voice that steers you toward good decisions in your life and away from bad ones. There is a mass of evidence that suggests that conscience, your moral sense, is a universal phenomenon and transcends all religions and boundaries. Immanuel Kant said, "I am constantly amazed by two things: the starry heavens above and the moral law within." Conscience, if educated properly, can become that moral law within. Some people believe, as author Stephen Covey does, that it is the voice of God to his children. When you listen to your conscience it drives your actions and reflects both the good in you and the good in others. It illuminates principles of honesty, fairness, integrity, love, kindness, and positive thoughts.

Conscience is a still, small voice within you, and it is associated with positive things. Ego, on the other hand, is driven by your social mirror and dictatorial. It focuses on the needs of self first and is not concerned with the well-being of others. It drives one to search to meet ends in any way, even if that way is underhanded, dirty, or duplicitous. Ego straightjackets potential and seeks to disempower others and is threatened by any negative feedback. It even punishes those who offer advice and feedback. Conscience is the opposite of ego; it values feedback as "feed forward" and seeks to empower and unleash the creativeness and innovating side in others.

This is simple. Listen to your conscience, and avoid your ego at all cost. Ego will cost you friends and loved ones. Begin today to live in congruence with your conscience. As your heart and mind steer you toward something, listen and act. This synergy between what is deeply important to you (conscience) and your actions will create alignment and congruence with your deepest source. At the end of the day, what we're really looking for is not peace of mind but peace of conscience. If we have a piece of conscience, we know internally that our external actions followed our deepest internal thoughts and are in alignment with who we really want to be, not what the world tells us we should become. Listening to this still, small voice will help you navigate the choppy waters of life and minimize regret later.

Find a Lifeline and Form Your Own Personal Board of Directors

Your life is sacred and important. Wise counsel can help you avoid a life of heartache and pitfalls. To help with major life planning as it relates to your personal life, professional life, financial matters, and direction, you should form your own personal board of directors (PBOD). This body should consist of people who are your advocates. The difference between an advocate and a friend is essential. An advocate has your back in all situations and would never do anything to devalue your relationship. An advocate will stand up for you when you are absent if others are negative about you, and an advocate will be the first to tell you if you are involved with things or people who could potentially harm your well-being. Much of friendships and relationships today are built around convenience. Friends may only be there for you when it's a good time for them, they may allow others to talk about you behind your back, and they may secretly wish for you to fail. They are not advocates for you.

Now that we've discussed the differences between advocates and friends, let's look at your board. Your board should have three to five members. These people should have many life experiences in both failure and defeat, and they should have both the character and competence you need to trust them at highly personal levels. They should have reached some level of success in their own lives, and they should be consistently back up what they say. Once they have built their integrity, you will trust their judgment. You will meet with these people as often as once a quarter, possibly over dinner, or a minimum of twice per year. Here are some areas you should discuss and seek guidance:

1. Career goals, redefining of those goals, and setting reasonable benchmarks
2. Relationships
3. Spirituality
4. Support for new challenges in your life
5. Grief periods after loss in your life
6. Motivation before embarking on new journeys
7. Financial matters
8. The open exchange of knowledge and wisdom

These are only eight, but I think they are a critical eight. Obviously you could call emergency meetings (just like a real board), but this is a time to listen up and take notes. Many of the true advocates we have in our life truly want us to be successful and will help navigate us down the uncertain waters in life. They care and want the best for us. Many times you will not want to hear what they have to say, but it is vitally important to create an environment where the truth is heard, and they don't simply tell you what you want to hear. These sessions should last anywhere from two to six hours and should be planned.

Start today by identifying your own board of directors and shave years off of your learning by avoiding the school of hard knocks. In life, we seldom exceed those with whom we are associated. When you get serious about achievement in your life, you start to build deep, meaningful relationships based on trust, vulnerability, generosity toward life and causes, and meaning and purpose. These lifeline relationships will stir your soul, help you bounce back from adversity, and challenge you to grow. This group has your back and you have theirs.

Redefine Feedback to "Feed Forward"
and Take It as a Gift

Part of making learning a way of being is to redefine what feedback is. Unfortunately, in our scarcity minded society, where we believe in win-lose thinking, much of the feedback that is given from one group to another is negative and construed that way. Because of that, we tend to tune it out as a personal attack on our character. When you're giving feedback, never attack the character of another person, but rather the behavior of that person. If we could redefine the word *feedback* to "feed forward" and search for the grains of truth in every comment we get from another, we become proactive to the words and not reactive.

Sure, there is some feedback that is malicious and has a negative connotation, but as we continue to educate ourselves, we see that everyone is approaching every situation from a unique perspective. Often the gaps in paradigms between two people allow for the biggest opportunities for disagreement. If we viewed those gaps as opportunities for synergy and creativity versus gaps of disagreement, we would be a whole lot better off.

Think of feedback as a gift. If viewed properly, that gift could be the best gift you ever receive. I will address this concept later when I discuss using adversity to accelerate progress (*Decision No. 5: Add Value Versus Subtract It*), but for a moment think about all the things said to you in your life that you found hurtful and resentful. I bet your heart was involved in those things. This could have come in the form of a significant other breaking up with you or a co-worker who you thought you had a great relationship with slamming you behind your back. Either way, it hurt. At the root of those comments could have been some truth that you did not recognize; it only illuminated the truth to you about the other person. You don't deserve to be in a relationship where the other person doesn't love you, and you do not want to have to count on someone who is not reliable because they do not believe in you.

Kelly Lavender, a dear friend and a very wise woman, frequently reminds me, "When people try and show you who they are, you should always believe them." And I tell people, "What you are shouts so loudly I cannot hear what you have to say." Either way, people are constantly showing us who they are and if we can trust them. Learn to change the picture about what feedback is, see it as a very valuable gift you need to know in order to move in the next direction. Make a decision to associate and spend your time only with people who have your best interest at heart. Then, you know that their feedback is for your best interest and not theirs.

When we build open and trusting environments, we understand that the feedback we offer and receive is there for one reason: to help us improve. Some people don't know how to appropriately offer feedback, but we should always listen to what people are saying, not how they say it. When we Make Learning a Way of Being we actively seek out coaches and mentors in our lives who we want to be brutally honest with us so we can experience important breakthroughs.

Build Your Team with People Who Are Smarter than You

How do you grow beyond your past limitations into new arenas of success? You have to expand, challenge your current way of thinking, and be willing to get out of the boat. One sure way to grow in any area of your life is to find and listen to as many smart people as you can. Set up monthly meetings with people where you can share knowledge and be inspired. I call these connector meetings, and I try and schedule a minimum of four of these each week. Remember, that word *inspire* means to breathe life into something, and in these meetings successful people can share their wisdom and knowledge with you. It's not enough to sit back and wonder how people became successful; we need to actively understand through firsthand knowledge how they got there so we can have our own ideas around our version of success.

There are certain people in my life who I meet with regularly in each arena where we share knowledge and ideas about current trends, what works and what doesn't, and discuss new techniques, principles, and strategies of success. In the coaching business I keep a network of the best that I can call to pick their brains. I have the same kind of people in the speaking and consulting business. These conversations illuminate and validate the belief and potential in what I'm doing. They usually stir something in me that awakens my inner fire. Just as a board of directors helps you both personally and professionally in certain general areas, these people are experts in their field and help you to grow your competence.

This is one important habit to cultivate. Stephen Covey (1989) calls it the habit of renewal, which he named "Sharpening the Saw." We must all learn to sharpen our saw in all dimensions including:

1. Body
2. Mind
3. Heart
4. Spirit

By listening and drinking deeply from the knowledge of others, we hone our own skills in all four dimensions. The next step is to take our newfound knowledge, act on it, and then share it with as many people as we can. Only scarcity-minded people hoard information, refusing to share it with others. Individuals who believe in abundance share with others everything they know. Start today by finding those smart people and listen up! This week sit down and write out four connectors you would like to meet with. Send them an e-mail to see when you can get on their schedule so you can share ideas. Tell them you have followed their success and would like an opportunity to sit and talk for a few minutes. Very few people will turn you down, unless you come across as unprepared and a waste of their time. Once you schedule the meetings, strive to articulate your value and differential advantages, because you now have a chance to shine and show them who you are, what you do, and why you matter.

LEARN MORNING, NOON, AND NIGHT

This is a very critical point to learning. To learn anything you must first become both humble and teachable and intentional. As a basketball coach, I am constantly saying, "The teacher cannot teach until the pupil is ready." This simply means that until a player is ready to be taught, no learning will occur. Many times in life we create the very adversity we are facing by being filled with venom and pride. Remember, "Pride goeth before a fall" (Proverbs 16:18). Pride stems from ego and is in direct contrast with conscience. When we believe that we know everything there is to know, that very thought limits our growth. Intelligent people understand that as our circle of knowledge grows so does our circle of ignorance. You see, the more we know, the more we realize we don't know. If you remember this concept you will be in a perpetual state of learning and growing, wanting to retain and act on as much information as possible.

The second you think you know everything or that you can't learn anything from another, you have created a roadblock to your learning. If you are in an organization and you are a leader in that organization, most likely you will want all of your people to learn and grow. The best example you can give to those people is to model the way. If you want them to learn, let them see you learn and grow. If you want them to become humble and teachable, let them see you being humble and teachable. Seek first the benefit of others versus your own benefit, and watch your relationships grow and expand. To become intentional about your learning I suggest this cycle (which I also subscribe to):

1. Read spiritual material in the morning. This gets your mind-set and perspective where it needs to be to tackle the day, gets you in a mind-set of gratitude, and opens up your heart and mind to becoming successful.
2. Read something specific in your field during the day (when you have breaks, while waiting at restaurants, when you are holding for something). I read business news during the day that sharpens my coaching skills and makes me more valuable to my clients.
3. Reward yourself at night by reading what you want. At night I treat myself to whatever I want in the form of books on a subject I'm interested, an autobiography or anything I want.

The point here is simple: make learning intentional and build it into the fabric of your life every day and in every way. You will seldom see me go anywhere without a book in my hand and a CD in my car. This curiosity quotient is critical to long-term success and making you stay relevant in your life and in your field.

EVERYBODY IS TRYING TO HELP US GET BETTER

They always tell us that when there is a fire, we should look, listen, and roll. Well, in this setting of listening and learning, you should also look, listen, and roll. Look at the example of others around you. Constantly study people and what makes them successful or unsuccessful. Read, listen, go to lectures, talk with others, watch body language, watch educational television, and constantly evaluate others.

Look to see what makes things work or not. Many times the answers come to us by watching others fail. Listen to those around you. Listen to wise counsel. Listen to your board of directors. Listen to your advocates. Listen to your inner voice. Just be quiet and listen. And finally, roll. Roll with the punches. Roll with adversity. Roll with setbacks. Roll with heartaches. Roll with negativity. Just roll with it!

The point here is simple: We live in an information-overloaded society. If you really want to grow and expand, the answers are simply all around you. All you have to do is listen and learn in order to grow and expand. Start today by listening and observing twice as much as you speak. We have two eyes and two ears and only one mouth for a reason. I think the Good Lord was trying to tell us something with that. Google has afforded us the opportunity to ask questions and find answers, and bookstores and libraries are filled with smart people who want to help us advance our lives. When I have questions about anything in life I look for answers. My first stop is the local bookstore. I gather all the information I can on the subject, and I focus in on the key learnings from each of those books so I can speak confidently on the matter. I became a leadership expert by immersing myself in a decade of deep leadership study, so I carved out a niche in the market by packaging my unique past experiences (championship basketball coach) with my unique learnings (leadership study) and built a unique process around both of those to create a process that is difficult to duplicate. This deep learning in your life can become your greatest competitive advantage if you choose to. You become the expert in the field, and people call you when they need help in that area. You offer solutions to the problems of the world.

DON'T LET YOUR JOB GET IN THE WAY OF YOUR CAREER

I come across so many people who have so many wonderful ideas about their lives. Between their thinking and their doing is often a space, and in that space lies their ability to choose their response to virtually any situation they have. (I will revisit turning thought into action with *Decision No. 7: Act or Be Acted Upon,* but for now, just think.) When I ask people to talk about their passion, they immediately speak from their hearts, because they are listening to their conscience.

Just this moment, as I look over the beautiful water outside Ketchikan, Alaska, on the way to Victoria, Canada, I am overwhelmed with passion. As I write, the words seem to flow naturally because I know that the contents will help people from all walks of life to act on their hopes and dreams and prevent them from living lives of quiet desperation. I know when I am speaking and coaching and consulting that I am right where I need to be at that moment. The joy and pleasure that I get from acting on my inner hopes brings both happiness and fulfillment to my life. It helps me to fully understand that this ain't no practice life and that we should all be able to fully experience passionate execution and significant contribution. We should all be able to wake up in the morning and go to a job we love for a cause we deem worthy and for a leader in whom we believe.

As we listen to our inner hearts and act from those intentions, we begin to create a synergy between our heart and our mind, and an inner peace both calms and excites at the same time. It is the ultimate synergistic process, what Covey calls "the sweet spot." Many of you have experienced this sweet spot in your vocations and can relate to what I am saying, but far too many have not found this sweet spot and long for it. By following the seven keys in this book, you are well on your way to living a life that matters because your life will be integrated around what you love.

Now that I have you where you need to be, I have to teach you how to reach your dreams. This process will always start by opening your mind and your heart to those inspirations in life that are trying to help you achieve inner peace by marrying your time and talents with a need in the world that only you can fulfill. By making learning a way of being, you initiate the process and become totally humble and teachable.

Chapter 5 Summary: Seven Action Items to Manifest Learning as a Way of Being

1. *Today,* I will stop, be completely quiet, and listen to my conscience. I will follow the inner wisdom of my conscience. Today, I will be fully aware of how I treat others and notice if that treatment is congruent with my inner spirit. I will seek to build others up rather than tear others down. I will seek to illuminate the potential in myself and in others. Today, I will reflect on life by asking what my conscience would do in every situation. I will then act from that still, small voice that points me toward right and away from wrong.

2. *Today,* I will begin to think about who I would like to join my board of directors. I will search for people who care deeply about me, illuminate the potential in me, and build me up. Today, I will seek to find and listen to these individuals who offer hope, faith, and wisdom and care deeply that I make good decisions in my life. I will form this board of directors with people who radiate the qualities I seek to create in my life. Today, I will pick up the phone and call a mentor, an advocate, or a teacher to seek wisdom and guidance in my life. One day I want to be on the board of directors for someone, so I will begin living with wisdom daily.

3. *Today,* I will seek and accept feedback as "feed forward." I will not associate people with their words and will only seek to listen with an intent to improve. Today, I will see adversity as my greatest

teacher, and I will value the negative things that happen in life. Today, I will seek not to judge others or assume motive, but rather to listen with my head and my heart in order to improve. The fact that I listen with an intent to improve will build credibility with others and will only grow my influence. Today, I will ask, "What can I do to help you?" and "What can I do to improve?" When I receive this feed forward, I will not judge or punish the messenger, but thank them for the message. I have the power to choose what I do with the information I gather.

4. *Today,* I will find and listen to as many smart people as I can. Today, I will go to the bookstore and buy a book in which I am interested. Today, I will pick up the phone and call that person who has the wisdom I am seeking. Today, I will go to that seminar I've been discussing. Today, I will see the day as a learning laboratory to glean as much information as I can. Today, I will create the action plan to continue my education in some capacity. Today, I will quit denying that knowledge gives me options and will seek that knowledge. Today, I will build a team around me that complements my weak points. I will not allow insecurity to stop me from building a world-class team.

5. *Today,* I will become humble and teachable. Today, I will fully comprehend that I do not want to fall victim to atrophy. Today, I will fully grasp that my mind's need is to learn and expand, and I can only do that when I become humble and teachable. Today, I will check my pride and ego at the door and become a sponge to the teaching of others. I will allow information and knowledge to inspire and uplift me. Today, I will grow my knowledge by realizing the first step on the path to education is to admit my ignorance. Today, I will model learning to everyone I associate with, and I will not attach formal titles to my assumptions of others'

knowledge bases. Today, I will learn from everyone, including children and peers.

6. *Today,* I will view my workday as a learning experience. Today, I will approach life and my job as an adventure that is fun and exciting. Today, I will open my mind and my heart to possibility. I will dream and hope again and believe again. Today, I will even learn from the mistakes of others in order to be sure not to repeat those mistakes. Today, I have decided to become a lifelong learner, and I will use every experience to sharpen my skills to be effective. Today, I will keep a book in my possession, a learning CD in my car, and a key area I want to learn in my heart and mind. Today, I will intentionally learn and grow in areas in which I am interested.

7. *Today,* I will listen to my internal compass as it relates to my vocation. I will fully understand the difference between an occupation and a vocation. I will no longer see my job as a means to a financial end, but rather as an opportunity to connect to my source, contribute meaning to the world, and effectively leave a legacy to those with whom I associate. Today, I will seek to detect my voice if I have not found it or share it with others if I have. Today, I will make a significant difference in the world. Today, I will be a creative force in the world. Today, I will get a peace of conscience by knowing I have cultivated my deepest potential in the world.

Chapter 6

Add Value Versus Subtract It

IN EVERY INTERACTION WE
EITHER ADD OR SUBTRACT VALUE

MANY PEOPLE TODAY SIMPLY do not want to pay the price or build the capacity to reach an aspiration. We live in a transactional quick-fix society of people who want things when they want them. They see every relationship only as a means to help them get what they want. Because of this mentality they often get to the top of the ladder of success only to learn that their achievement caused tremendous damage and broken relationships along the way. They regret their ascension to the top and talk about the emptiness in their lives and wish they could go back and do it all over again. In their second attempt they would make a fundamental change in their behavior. They would always add value to the lives of those they care about rather than subtract it.

We hear so many people talk about the goals they need for their life. They spend valuable time and energy talking about what they want to do, but they seldom act on those conversations, which leads only to short-term cotton-candy satisfaction versus long-term fulfillment. I tell people that the word *goal* is one of the most overused

135

words and underdone achievements in America. Think about your own life. When was the last time you took the time and energy to think (vision) about where you are and where you want to go (discipline)? Stopping to think alone is more than most Americans ever attempt. To go somewhere, you must reflect on where you are, and this takes pausing in life to study, investigate, feel, think, understand the true context of your current situation, and accept it as it is.

Many people begin each year with a list of New Year's resolutions and then decide not to change because it is just too hard or because of some other perceived roadblock. Think about this as it relates to goals. The word *January* derives from the Greek goddess Janus who had two faces, one that looks backward to reflect on the past, and one that looks forward to focus on the future; thus January means new beginning. In the beginning, people want to change, reach a new level of success, or become inspired to create prosperity in life, but then the gravitational pull of society pulls them back down.

My point is simple: study where you currently are, and instead of trying to sell something, start adding so much value that people cannot do without you. Become irreplaceable, indispensable. Become a "must have" rather than a "nice to have." By using the decision of adding value versus subtracting it, you begin to understand that there is a process to achievement and significance, and that process cannot be denied.

The quickest way to get from where you are to where you would like to be is by building, acquiring, and strengthening the relationships in your life. This is one reason I built the Legacy Management System, which focuses on building relationships in five key areas:

1. The Target 25 (advocates who love you)
2. The Suspect Pond (people who you want to do business with or move into your top tier)

3. Connectors (those you need to connect with in order to build a relationship)
4. Leads (those who have contacted you with a cue, bump, or invite that they need help)
5. Net Promoters (those who are actively promoting you and who come out of your strengthening relationships with your current clients)

The model is simple: build and acquire new relationships across the country by adding value to them first and anticipating their needs.

In this chapter I outline seven key principles and processes that you must go through and experience in order to reach the level of significance you've been talking about. Remember this: vision without execution is only hallucination.

Every Day at Your Current Job Is an Interview for Your Next Job

At eighteen years old I went back to the elementary school I attended and told the principal I wanted to coach basketball. He looked at me and said it would not happen because I was only eighteen. I was adamant about my passion for the game and finally convinced him I was worthy and had the conviction to do it. He teamed me with an adult, and we co-coached that team to a state championship in our first year and a state runner-up in year two. That one decision was a defining moment and flashpoint in my life.

I used the very concepts I have discussed in this book to continue to climb the ladder to where I am today. That decision was important because I understood the concept that every day at your current job is an interview for you next job. When I was coaching that elementary team I wore a suit and treated every day like I was in the big time. That led to my next assignment as an assistant at one of the largest high schools in Tennessee at the age of nineteen. I was named the head freshman coach while I was in college and used that time (from age nineteen to twenty-one) to grow my influence with everyone at the school and earn my keep. That led to my taking over as the head coach of the women's program at age twenty-two, when I was named the youngest head coach in the state of Tennessee. At age thirty-one I became one of the youngest athletic directors in Tennessee, and after winning a championship, I retired to chase my dream of impacting people around the world.

If you approach your current job as an interview for your next job, you will work every day with a passion, purpose, and focused intention toward improvement. When you do this, people will notice and you will grow your influence and begin to move up in the world. Many people stagnate in their jobs, become complacent, and then complain to others that they are unhappy and cannot move up in the company. You've got to work at the outside edge of your influence by taking the initiative on your own to grow these things. Too many people just sit and wait for something to happen to them. You have to make things happen, and the first step toward doing that is to think there is always something bigger out there for you than where you currently are.

Practice *Key No. 2* and begin to design your own dream. When you become intentional about where you are, you expand your possibilities for where you can go. Just as ever day at your current job is an interview for your next job, every day with your current customer is an interview for your next customer.

THE PRICE MUST BE PAID AND THE PROCESS MUST BE FOLLOWED: THERE ARE NO SHORTCUTS

During my lectures, I ask the audience if it is possible to get both a high school and college diploma and still not be educated? The common response is yes. You can cheat your way through both situations and still not be educated. But you really did not cheat the process, because you do not have the knowledge to be successful in the world.

The law of the harvest factors into everything as it relates to success. Farmers understand this better than anyone. When you plant seeds, they must be gardened with proper sunlight, water, and tending over a period of time. Without these simple things there will be no crop. Success is exactly the same way. What you sow is what you reap, and you must pay the price and go through the process in order to become successful.

Too many people today go for the "wealth without work" approach to success. This is an illusion. The going rate for any worthwhile win in today's society is ten good setbacks. That means you may fail ten times before you eventually get to where you are going. The only real difference between successful people and other folks is that some fall out of contention after only a few failures.

If you understand this concept, you approach failure as learning opportunities and steppingstones to future successes. If you try to cheat the process, you may reach some level of success, but you will most likely fall short of true significance, which is what I think most of us are living for. Understand that there will be many setbacks on the road to success, the price must be paid, and the process must be followed. Natural principles govern our world, so what you put in you will most likely get in return. This applies to both relationships and work.

Have you ever tried to quick fix an important relationship with some technique or strategy? Most likely the other person saw right through that façade, and you actually destroyed trust rather than build any. Begin today by not trying to shortcut your way to the top. Value your time at the bottom or middle of the ladder of success. It will help you to understand how to help other people when you get in a position of influence, and you will only reach a level of influence if you understand the law of the harvest.

WATER WHAT YOU WANT TO GROW

This is self-explanatory and common sense. Unfortunately, common sense is not always common practice. To continue the climb in your life, you must constantly tend to your garden. This applies to sharpening your skills, continuing to grow and expand, and challenging the process along the way. Let's take the first concept of sharpening your skills. Here are some key concepts to gardening your garden along the journey to the top.

1. Take care of your four dimensions:
    a. Body: Exercise regularly and always present yourself in a professional manner.
    b. Mind: Sharpen your mind by becoming a continual learner.
    c. Heart: Mend the relationships in your life that are strained and begin practicing not judging others.
    d. Spirit: Connect to meaningful projects in your life where you can pour out you heart and soul.
2. Continue to grow and expand and challenge the process.
    a. Challenge the current ways you think and see things by asking why you believe the way you do.
    b. Complete a life inventory to see where you are and where you are going.
    c. Listen with an open mind and an open heart to concepts and ideas that are in direct contrast to you.
    d. Become humble and teachable and realize that you do not know everything.

As you garden your garden, you will be making yourself marketable to the rest of the world because you will be a hot commodity and will be seen as an asset to any organization and a solution to the problems that many industries face. The marketplace needs people who are solutions oriented, not problem oriented. Seek to become the answers to the problems, rather than contribute to the problems, and watch your stock rise. Once you obtain the job you want, think in terms of what you can do for the company versus what the company can do for you, and you will begin to expand your influence.

Not long ago in my office at my home I wrote this statement on my white board: "Stop selling and start being the solution." When we pay the price and water what we want to grow in our lives, we become solutions oriented and add tremendous value to the world. Always remember, the bigger the contribution, the bigger the reward. If you're not currently satisfied with the reward the world is giving you, step back and look at your contribution. Earlier I noted that if we want a new outcome in life, we needed a new preparation and a new contribution. Our old contributions will not get us bigger rewards or bigger checks.

Each Step Offers a New Perspective: You're Only at a Rise, Not the Summit

When Stephen Covey began to write the bestseller *The 8th Habit,* he said in the acknowledgments that, because of a lifetime of teaching leadership and organizational effectiveness, he thought it would take only six months to write the book. He stated that one of the great learnings of his life was that if you wanted to make a new contribution, you have to make a whole new preparation (see *Decision No. 1: Experience an Awakening*). To go beyond the past you must cultivate a new paradigm, a new perspective.

After a year of teaching and writing, Covey and his team finished a rough draft. They were thrilled that they finally had arrived. Covey said, "It was at that moment we experienced what hikers often discover when climbing mountains. We hadn't reached the summit at all, only the top of the first rise." From that vantage point they could see things they had never seen before in ways they had never thought before. Covey went through that process of getting to a new rise nearly a dozen times until they finally reached the summit and finished the book five years later.

I can identify with this climb. I initially began writing this book more than three years ago, and I spoke on many of the concepts in over eighty speaking engagements around the world until I finally found the keys I was looking for. Those keys were what I referred to at the time as the Seven Principles of Success. I was convinced that they offered the framework I was searching for to complete this book. When I was on vacation in Alaska, I found just what I was looking for: time and inspiration.

As you climb the ladder of success, after a lot of hard work and commitment, you will believe that you have reached your destination. But you will have reached a new rise where you can see new things that you could never see before. Truthfully, I don't know if we ever get to the top, but each rise is very rewarding, and in the end it's the climb that will be the most memorable. Cherish those rises and continue to climb that mountain.

Go Looking for Answers on the Inside of Your Life

In life you need a healthy, investigative awareness about what is working and what is not. Many people unfortunately develop a functional blindness to their defects and shortcomings and never fully sharpen their perception through investigation into whether their strategies are working or not. This is the part of the book that I'm going to ask you the infamous question that Dr. Phil asks his guests: "How's that working out for you?" I have seen too many people continue to do things for years that never work. I have seen people stay in jobs, in relationships, in misery for years because of two things: an inability to confront the brutal facts and an inability to act on what they know.

Tara Bennett-Goleman (2001) wrote in *Emotional Alchemy,* "If we see only through the lens of our assumptions—our thoughts and beliefs—we are not in touch with how these lenses distort the reality of the moment." By constantly analyzing all parts of your life through this sharpening of your investigative skills you are completing the cycle of the Belief and Action model mentioned at the beginning of the book. The cycle ends with reflection on what is working and not working in your life, and it begins again and is never ending, because you can change what is not working.

Begin to study your life, both personally and professionally with an intent to learn, grow, and be challenged by the process so you can become better. Remember to accept feedback as a gift that will help you reach the next level in your life. In my lectures I call this "completing an autopsy." I borrowed the terminology from Jim Collins in *Good to Great.* As you complete autopsies on your life of both the good and the bad, you create an environment in your head and in your heart where the truth can be heard and not filtered. This gives you an accurate barometer and gauge to work with for future decisions. It is only after we are willing to reflect on the actuality of our life can we accept situations as they are and make the necessary improvements for the future.

Every week my team has what I call the Monday and the Friday. On Monday I add value to my team by discussing one key teaching point I'm using to help them win that week. We have a long discussion about processes, ideas, and game changers. On Friday we reassemble at my pool for a success party. We discuss the wins and losses of the week and what we have coming up, so we can focus our energy toward our dominant aspiration. This concept of continual involvement in one another's lives builds positive energy and makes generous deposits in the emotional bank accounts of those people with whom I work. Start your own Monday and Friday schedule to discuss where you're going (vision) and the progress your making toward getting there.

THERE'S ONLY ONE WAY TO USE ADVERSITY, AND THAT'S TO ACCELERATE PROGRESS

In the very beginning of this book I mentioned that there were several common themes that I found from people in all walks of life as I have traveled the country. The first was the gap between thinking and doing, or what I refer to as the execution gap. This is common among organizations as well. The second common theme is that all people and all organizations will face some level of adversity. We do not know what level of adversity that will be, but we can rest assured that it will be there. How can we spur people to act on what they think versus merely talk about it? How can we use adversity in our lives to accelerate progress instead of little or no movement toward taking positive action?

One year, in the middle of our basketball season, three of my best players were injured. All the people following our program believed we were finished, but not me. I sat down with my staff and said we have to come up with a way to use this adversity to our benefit in a way to propel us toward a new level rather than paralyze us with fear and anxiety. We devised a five-point plan to transform this adversity into progress, and I have been teaching that plan ever since. It is outlined in the next subheading. The point here is a big one. If we know that unfortunate things are going to happen to us, don't you think it would be wise to decide today that we are going to use those things to our benefit rather than our detriment? This simple concept will become very powerful in your life as you meet challenges and will most likely separate the contenders from the pretenders.

Life really is about one degree of separation from other people, especially in competitive markets. By using the perceived bad things in life to produce good things, you may very well be on your way to creating that separation between you and your competitors. Unfortunately, we create 90 percent of the adversity we face in life by our own actions or inactions. Backtrack some of the messes you have gotten yourself in, and tell me you didn't have a hand in creating them. We must ask some hard questions when we struggle, but we must understand that if we went back thousands of years in the past or journeyed thousands of years into the future, there would be only two constants: opportunity and struggle. How we utilize them determines our quality of life in every stream of our lives.

You Need to Have a Plan to Use Adversity When It Arises

When you have a plan, you are prepared to meet the unexpected. Knowing that we live in a permanent whitewater society where the only constant is change, I feel it is very important to have a mind-set, a paradigm, and a plan to meet that sea of change. This plan will help you to create a mental model to use every time something bad happens in your life. It will most certainly help you to view those negative things as learning experiences. I have taught this plan to people in all walks of life. It has universal meaning and applicability. Here are the five steps:

1. Replace the question "Why is this happening to me or us?" with "What is this trying to teach me or us?"
2. Ask "What was my contribution to this adversity?"
3. Get stable. You can't make good decisions when you're irrational.
4. Get help. There are people close to you who have more to give than what they're giving. We have an enormous capacity to act when needed and enormous reservoirs of untapped potential if we need it.

5. Act. The unwanted outcome happened in the past. Don't let that snapshot determine your future.

As mentioned earlier, the Organization of Victimization did a study of people who had some serious adversity in their lives (cancer patients, prisoners of war, traumatic car accidents) to see how they responded. They findings revealed the following:

1. One group of people was permanently dispirited by the adversity. They never returned to normal.
2. The second group returned to normal, but that was it.
3. The third group used the event as a defining moment in their lives to become better than they were before the event happened.

When adversity hits you, which group will you fall into? Remember, there is a space between every stimulus in your life and your response to it. In that space lies your ability to choose your response. When you understand this, you realize that in the end you create the stimuli with your response to it. By using adversity to accelerate progress in your life, there are no bad experiences, only learning experiences. If you take this approach, there is also no failure, only experience. This simple concept will go very far in helping you to live a life of deep meaning and significant contribution because you will value each step of the process. There will be no bad days, only good days filled with learning and growth en route toward a destination.

Chapter 6 Summary: Seven Action Items to Manifest the Decision to Add Value Versus Subtract It

1. *Today,* I will work with intent, purpose, presence, and passion at my current job because I know that I have an opportunity to build

advocates and make a difference. Today, I will fully understand that I am not where I need to be on the way to getting there. Today, I will evaluate my current situation and work to improve it. Today, I will understand that I am a solution to the challenges I face in the workplace, and I will work to grow my influence with others and improve their perceptions of me. Today, I will serve human needs in principle-centered ways.

2. *Today,* I will fully understand that there are natural laws and principles that govern life. I will understand that there is no quick way to become successful and that every worthwhile goal I plan to achieve will take time, patience, persistence, and perseverance. Today, I will work to sow good things, which I will tend daily with a singleness of purpose toward my destination. Today, I will become the change I seek to create in the world by matching my internal thoughts with external action. Today, I will pay the price to be successful and seek to only add value in every interaction with others versus subtract it.

3. *Today,* I will water what I want to grow. Today, I will decide what the most important things in my life are, and I will invest my time and energy in alignment with those things. Today, I will understand that true achievement and significance begins with the seed of a dream and belief and only manifests by connecting to a source and working diligently in the direction of those dreams. Today, I will cultivate the discipline to act daily around my highest priorities, and I will focus on execution.

4. *Today,* I will stop and take a moment to view where I currently stand in life and where I want to go. I will work fervently to climb the mountain of success, realizing that I may never get there but that each rise will help me to see life in new, exciting ways. Today, I

will value where I am, but I will not be satisfied with staying here. Today, I will pack the tools I need to climb the mountain and focus on placing the right tools in my luggage. Today, I will learn new skills to take with me along the journey and will not discount anyone else's ideas, because I may be able to use them in the future.

5. *Today*, I will investigate my current way of thinking and living and see where I am aligned with my conscience. Today, I will realize that the pressures of life and our win-lose society will only hinder and hold me back from realizing my potential if I allow it to. Today, I will sharpen my perception of the world in which I operate, and I will seek first the benefit of those around me rather than my own benefit. Today, I will become a continual evaluator of my life and how my actions affect others. Today, I will enter the college of studying my thoughts, my tendencies, and my actions.

6. *Today*, I will value adversity. Today, I will understand that adversity can become an event that causes me to study current ways of thinking and doing that are unproductive. Today, I will understand that adversity can make me stronger, make me value things I have neglected, and make me express my love for others. Today, I will not need adversity to teach me that I should be thankful for my current situation and for the people in my life. Today, I will use any adversity to accelerate progress versus little or no movement. Today, I will be thankful that adversity has taught me some of the most valuable lessons of my life.

7. *Today*, I will create a plan to use perceived negative experiences in my life for benefit rather than harm. Today, I will understand that the key to successful living is through wisdom, and I can only gather wisdom through experience. Today, I will use the very adversity that paralyzes some to create improvement in my life. Today, I will value adversity.

Chapter 7

Build Up Versus Tear Down

MAKE A CONSCIOUS CHOICE TO ACT IN ABUNDANCE RATHER THAN SCARCITY

AS WE BEGIN TO grow and mature, we come to understand some simple principles. The rent we pay for living on this earth is paid by our service to others. As we climb the emotional ladder, we also comprehend that the best way to achieve significant, sustainable significance in life is by losing ourselves in service to others. Lately, I have come to realize that a great life is one that is built around inspired living and trying to achieve an everyday greatness. One common theme that continues to surface in my life is that of being true to principle and not allowing the negative undertone of the world or scarcity-minded people to control my hopes or dreams. People should always get the best version of you versus some representative of you that acts from personality rather than true character.

This sixth decision is built around an abundant paradigm that teaches us that there is enough in the world for us to have all we want without ever having to take away from another or be jealous of the success of another. This is in stark contrast to the prevalent mind-set of most people who are deeply rooted in win-lose thinking, almost obsessed with confessing the sins of others, and making excuses or rationalizing why they do not have a bigger piece of the pie. This key teaches us that if you really want to be successful, you will help other people to be successful.

A nice habit to cultivate as it relates to practicing this decision is to constantly search for opportunities to build others up rather than tear others down. Practice tolerance for other people's views and opinions, and do not become easily offended if those views are not in alignment with yours. Listen with intent to understand versus intent to reply, and truly seek the benefit of others first versus your own benefit. In essence, build and think in terms of service and contributing to the greater good. In the process, a funny thing will happen: others will return to you what you project to the world.

In every interaction and in every way, we have a chance to build others up, and sometimes the greatest gift we can offer is the gift of honesty and authenticity that we want others to be successful in every way. We are never in competition with others, but rather with our own tiny potential, therefore we can let down our guard and genuinely be happy for the successes of others.

UNDERSTAND ABUNDANCE VERSUS SCARCITY

As you move from interdependent thinking into the interdependent realities of the world, you begin to realize that the only way to true significance is by co-missioning with others. It is through synergy and the combination of talents that we negate our weaknesses and build on our strengths and the strengths of others to reach our destination. To do this effectively we must learn to think in ways of abundance versus scarcity. Let me illustrate the two paradigms.

Scarcity-minded thinking stems from a paradigm of control and fear, where one believes that in order to succeed in life, she must do so at the expense of others. She believes that there is only one pie, and if others get a piece, then there will not be any left for her. She has hidden agendas and is undermines, backstabs, pulls down, compares, contends, criticizes, competes, and politicks. This is not a category you want to be in, but it is one most people live in. This negative cycle begins at an early age and becomes apparent later in life. If you don't believe me, just watch a peewee football, basketball, or baseball game. The parents focus on the benefit of one—their child—versus the benefit of all. This type of thinking continues to build an individualistic paradigm around competing with others for a sense of self-worth and potential.

A strong sense of self-awareness is needed to overcome this type of negative thinking and become genuinely happy for the successes of the group. Life is interdependent, not independent. The faster we teach young people this through modeling, the more tolerance we will build, the more unity we will build, and the more fulfillment we will build. The question becomes where does this scarcity-minded thinking stem from that is deeply scripted into us. Naturally, we are led to believe it comes from our upbringing, our environments, and what we have been fed in our minds. This is why the great Baptist preacher Dr. Charles Stanley said, "We always reap what we sow, more than we sow it, for longer than it was sown." In essence, what was fed into our lives early in our lives comes to harvest later in our lives. Scarcity-minded thinking is deep within us and comes from our parents; they did not know there was a better way of thinking and believed in a win-lose mind-set.

Abundance-mentality thinking stems from a paradigm of abundance, infinite possibilities, and unlimited opportunities. This person believes that there is enough success and happiness out there for everyone to have all they want without competing, criticizing, or comparing himself to others. This person believes in the potential and worth of others and is sincerely happy for the success of others. He also understands the concept, "If you want to retain those who are present, be loyal to those who are absent." Therefore, he does not speak negatively or enable the bad-mouthing of others when they are not present.

This is where most people want to live, but they allow circumstances, environment, or the gravitational pull of an individualistic society to pull them into scarcity thinking. Abundance is like air; it's infinite and everywhere. Just as air is everywhere, so are the opportunities to manifest your future. Abundance-minded people spend their days adding value to others versus subtracting it in needless drama or by becoming an emotional cancer. They use every interaction as an opportunity to deepen relationships and always make the most of every situation, because they understand that people are perfectly aligned to get the results they are getting.

As you can see, it is clear which mind-set you should live from. If it is that easy, then why do so many people operate from a scarcity mind-set? That answer is fairly simple to me. We live in such a competitive win-lose society that we are taught from an early age that we must compare ourselves with others, we must step over to get ahead, and we must climb the ladder of success at all cost. The real key to achievement and significance is through others. Study history and all major success stories of moral authority, and you will find that only through the movement of a group did anything large ever get accomplished. One person might have been the catalyst to start the movement, but others have to be enlisted to make the major contributions.

This brings me back to a point I made earlier in the book, that of a trim-tabber. A trim-tab is the small rudder on the big rudder of a boat or ship that turns the whole vessel. This small piece, when it moves, moves the big piece that in turn moves the entire thing. A person of great influence can be a trim-tabber, someone whose one movement moves the whole organization or possibly even a whole civilization.

Keep in mind, nothing happens until something moves. You be the person who takes the initiative to move in the direction of significance. If you want to achieve everyday greatness, stop being so concerned about who will get the credit and ante up what you can bring to the team. The first step is to listen to the words you use around others and determine where the ulterior motives come from. Most likely your language will tell you if you have an open mind and heart or a competitive mind and heart.

GET INTENTIONAL ABOUT BEING TAUGHT

In life there are opportunities to share one's knowledge, skills, and soul with others. As we begin to move up the ladder of interdependence and fully understand this concept of building others up, we search for those opportunities to share with others. I noted earlier in the book that we should develop our gifts and give them away to as many people as we can. In essence that is exactly what I am doing by speaking and writing, but this comes in a variety of forms for people everywhere. It could be a crucial conversation with a friend, a family member, a constituent, a co-worker, or a stranger.

As a coach and athletic director, I searched for opportunities to connect my voice (calling in life) with a touch during a conversation with others. I am constantly searching for the right opportunity to convey my appreciation and affirm and validate the worth and potential in others in clear ways so they begin to see it in themselves. Sometimes the best conversations are those where there is no talking at all, only silent communication, where feelings are so strong that you can sense the other person expressing love, disappointment, hurt, or anger.

When Phil Jackson was coaching the Chicago Bulls, he remembered a time when the infamous Dennis Rodman visited Jackson's Montana ranch. He said they sat for hours without talking at all. He could sense Dennis's anxiety and frustration that no one had ever understood him. The communication that day sealed the deal for

Dennis to play for Jackson and to help the Bulls go on to win a championship.

If you open your mind and spirit, you can sense what is going on with another person and when you should offer a word of encouragement. People give us many cues daily. For the best book on listening and offering help, read Bruce Wilkerson's *You Were Born for This* (2010).

These crucial conversations will put enormous deposits in the emotional bank accounts of others and will build your trust account in ways that are immeasurable. The people we associate with the most have to be affirmed the most because the expectations of the relationship are so much higher. Begin today to search for opportunities to build others up rather than participate in the negativity and reactiveness of tearing others down. This will lead to meaning and satisfaction versus a profound misalignment with your conscience. When you participate in the negativity that is so pervasive today, you become part of the problems of society rather than a part of the solution. This creates an inner animosity with your soul that will ultimately lead to unhappiness.

REDEFINE LEADERSHIP IN A NEW ERA

To reach any level of success, there must be a constant, continual, repetitive reinforcement of belief. In essence, you help people engage in a set of consistent and repetitive behaviors today that allows them to do something tomorrow they simply cannot do today. You must continue to confirm, validate, appreciate, and inspire those around you—beginning with yourself. Remember, those whom we associate with the most need the most deposits. As we reaffirm the potential and worth in others, we are expressing our voices and inspiring others to find their voices in the process. To revisit an earlier concept in the book you express your voice in four unique ways:

1. Vision: You see a better world for you and your group through your mind's eye.
2. Discipline: You become a disciple to other people as well as the cause you deem worthy. You affirm that belief and discipline to others.
3. Passion: You have the inner drive and intrinsic motivation to complete the journey with fire and enthusiasm.
4. Conscience: You move in the direction of your dreams and are guided by a deep need and longing to live a life of significance.

Notice how this repetitive cycle focuses on the whole person of your four dimensions:

1. Vision: Mind
2. Discipline: Body
3. Passion: Heart
4. Conscience: Spirit

By expressing your voice to others, you embark upon a journey toward significance, and you have the road map to complete the mission. As you live out of your imagination and attach your actions with integrity (which means living an integrated life around positive principles in the totality of your life) you work in principle-centered ways that produce an alignment with your inner core or spirit. This will lead to more happiness and fulfillment in your personal and professional life. Continue to reinforce your beliefs with your actions and your words so that others see you as legitimate and sincere about your efforts.

In an age of wisdom we need to redefine leadership in such a way that lights the fire of others and inspires them to unlock their potential versus managing people like things. We can have an idea and take it to its logical conclusion, and that can be called motivation. It's a pit-bull mentality. Inspiration is where the idea has a hold on us and takes us to the place we intend to be. Dr. Wayne Dyer taught me this great principle: our goal as leaders is to unlock rather than restrict.

TO BUILD OTHERS, YOU MUST FIRST BUILD
YOURSELF IN ALL FOUR DIMENSIONS

To build others up, you must first get to a place in your life so that you have the capacity to help others. You must first find your unique voice before you can inspire others to find theirs. You must develop your gift before you will have the capacity to give that gift away. If you work from a place of depleted energy, it will be difficult to light the fire of another. To do this you need a holistic approach toward developing the four capacities or four intelligences that derive from your four dimensions. You must build:

1. IQ (Intelligent Quotient): Mind
2. EQ (Emotional Intelligence): Heart
3. PQ (Physical Intelligence): Body
4. SQ (Spiritual Intelligence): Spirit

Remember the four needs of the complete person:

1. To live (body)
2. To learn (mind)
3. To love (heart)
4. To leave a legacy (spirit)

As you understand this, you begin to build the capacity in all four areas, making you a well-rounded, complete person who has the intelligence to compete in a global economy. In essence, you become a commodity to the world because of your knowledge, skills, desire, and beliefs. So many people who I speak to around the country are simply unhappy and feel that they have so much more to give in both their personal and professional lives. They are frustrated (misguided enthusiasm) and intimidated and are searching for answers to live an integrated life. This model of the whole person gives a complete picture from which to work. When all four dimensions are clicking in a profession, you are well on your way to doing what you love and loving what you do, which is in direct contrast to upward of 70 percent of most Americans who do not enjoy their professional careers and are unhappy with their personal lives.

Here are a few suggestions for developing the four capacities to meet the realities of the knowledge-worker era:

1. For the mind: Read, grow, expand, challenge yourself in multiple dimensions.
2. For the heart: Mend relationships, see the good in others, affirm the potential in others, and build up others versus tearing them down. Practice abundance versus scarcity.
3. For the body: Practice consistent, repetitive exercise. Eat healthy and value yourself.
4. For the Spirit: Connect to your inner core, find a cause to believe in, lose yourself in service to others, and practice a weekly or daily spirituality.

Once you cultivate and build the internal discipline to these four capacities, you will grow your influence with yourself and others. Have you ever seen someone who tried to lead when they were flawed with duplicity, poor character, inability to make and keep commitments, or physically a mess? The internal strength you build will carry over and flow into all areas of your life, making you an integrated person.

Specific Strategies for Building Up

I believe that good leaders affirm the worth and potential in others so clearly that they pull the best out. Think about your own life. Were there not people who separated your conditions or poor attitudes from your future potential and communicated that to you? They believed in the good of you when it was easy to see the bad. They helped you find your voice.

I think back to one of my first speaking engagements, when David Forrest walked up to me and said I should go on the circuit because of my talents. I think back to Marc LaBlanc, who at an Achiever's Circle in 2003 told me I should write a book. At that time, they saw something in me that I did not, and that affirmation kick-started the process of my discovering my voice. Those two instances took place in a single day. They were transformational. As you interact with others, you begin to see their potential and validate and communicate that potential to them. I am afforded the opportunity all the time as a coach and speaker, but you can find endless opportunities to build up the confidence of others in your daily interactions with the people around you.

One of my favorite stories is about a blind horse named Dusty. I heard Lou Holtz tell it many years ago. It illustrates the power of building people up to make them believe they are better than they really are.

Lou was driving in the country one day when he accidentally ran off the road. Cell phones didn't work in that part of the country, so his only choice was to ask a stranger up the road to help him out. The man had a barn out back and said he had a blind horse named Dusty, but they could hook Dusty up to the car and try to pull it out. Desperate, Lou took the man up on his offer.

After they hooked up Dusty, the farmer said, "Pull, Star! Pull!"

Dusty didn't move.

The man yelled out, "Pull, Charlie! Pull!"

Dusty just stayed put.

Lou began to think this guy was crazy and possibly psychotic.

Then the man said, "Pull, Dallas! Pull!"

Again Dusty didn't move.

Then the man yelled, "Pull, Dusty! Pull!"

With a mighty heave and a ho, Dusty pulled the car back on to the roadway.

Lou was excited but also confused. He said, "I really appreciate the help, but I don't quite understand. You called three different horses' names before you called out Dusty's. What was that about?"

The farmer said, "Are you kidding? Dusty is blind, not deaf. If he thought he had to do all that work by himself, he never would have tried it."

Sometimes you have to make others believe they have four horsepower when they only have one. Limiting yourself in your own mind will get you absolutely nowhere. How will other people believe in you and your abilities if you don't believe in yourself? Confidence is one of the key factors in manifesting the life you want. Identify those roadblocks in your mind today and start acting like the person you want to be versus the one you have always been. Sometimes the way you see the problem is the problem.

Regardless of the way you have been scripted by your parents (genetic determinism), you can effectively become a transition person, one who goes beyond past limitations and boundaries and changes the situation for the future. Here are five key points and ways to build other people up:

1. In every interaction, compliment another person quickly.
2. In every e-mail, always start with a pleasant word and thought.
3. In difficult times, always be the first to call or offer your services.

4. Lose yourself in other people's causes and dreams, and they'll lose themselves in yours.
5. Always be the one who makes and keeps your commitments to others. Even the smallest commitments.

DRAMA IS EVERYWHERE—CHOOSE NOT TO PARTICIPATE

In life you always have a choice about what you participate in. Anyone can certainly be negative, but you need to ask yourself, What has being negative ever gotten me? In my own life, going negative has either left me embarrassed or ashamed and usually put me in a lose-lose situation. As it relates to building others up and illuminating the good in others, there is simply no room for going negative and participating in the needless drama that so many people thrive on. Each of us has a certain amount of energy for the day, and we get to decide where we place and how we use that energy. We can choose to participate in areas that drain our energy or pit us in power struggles that result in broken relationships that may never heal and become constant sore spots that deplete energy.

When I first started coaching at the age of fifteen I thought I had to go negative when I became intense. The behavior was usually rewarded by winning, so I believed that going negative worked. Then I became educated. Just two years ago, my friend Randy Coffman taught me a valuable lesson: you can remain positive *and* still be intense. I call it the value of *and*.

Many times we simply see things in black and white. We cannot see the two sides, only the one side that leaves us locked in a creativity prison based on our past scripting. If you can begin to embrace the power of *and*, you can see that you can have two opposing things at once if you just open your mind and choose to see it.

I try my best not to participate in the negativity that only stifles growth and builds division among people. If we can just embrace the fact that others can be successful too, we can actually be happy for their successes rather than jealous of what they have to offer. Remember, jealously stems from a paradigm of fear and insecurity and manifests itself in terms of pulling others down, backstabbing, or going negative.

If you really want to maximize your potential, start by understanding that we are all one group of people on the same journey in search of the same thing: meaning. Choose today not to participate in the negativity and to become a light that illuminates the good in others. It will be one of the best decisions you will ever make.

Some people thrive on drama. If there is none, they will create it. Once you recognize these tendencies in others began to distance yourself from them. Sometimes these people are co-workers; sometimes they're your bosses. You must learn to conserve your good energy and not disempower yourself and allow another's weaknesses to control you. As I noted earlier, we only get twenty-five thousand mornings to wake up, so why waste a precious day on needless drama. Your life will be a whole lot better if you check that at the gate. When it arises, you should move in another direction.

Three Strategies to Always Add More Value

When you build up others you seek their benefit before your own benefit. Through the power of intention this will most likely attract a flow of positive energy from others who see the good in you. In tense situations where emotions are high and people believe strongly in one thing or another, I have found it useful to practice the three key habits of synergy, which were first introduced to me by my favorite author, Dr. Stephen Covey.

Habit no. 1: *Think in terms of Win-Win versus Win-Lose.* Search for alternatives where each person wins. Go the extra mile to ensure that others get what they want out of the situation.

Habit no. 2: *Seek first the benefit of others versus your own benefit.* Truly listen and feel with a sincere intent to walk in the shoes of another. Detach yourself from your current role and view life through the lens of another. I call this "paradigm trading," where you really try to see things from another person's perspective.

Habit no. 3: *Search for third alternatives.* Too many times in life we simply think in win-lose mind-sets. This is a natural manifestation of the competition-based identities scripted and shaped into us as children. Go to the table with an open mind and an open heart and practice each one of these key habits and chances are you will find a solution to the challenge you are facing.

Chapter 7 Summary: Seven Action Items to Manifest the Decision of Building Up Versus Tearing Down

1. *Today,* I will believe and act in abundance rather than scarcity. Today, just as the universe and the air are infinite and abundant, so too will my possibilities become infinite and abundant. Today, I will live inspired and be inspirational to others because I will seek to build up versus tear down. Today, I will become aware of my insecurities and jealousies and seek to transform them into confidence, belief, and hope for others. Today, I will begin to build people up in my daily interactions with others and will not waste precious energy on negative people.

2. *Today,* I will search for teachable opportunities with others. I will realize that others will become open, humble, and vulnerable to me when I am open, humble, and vulnerable to them. Today, I will view life as an upward spiral of learning and growing, and I will approach each day with an intent to grow my knowledge, skills, desire, and belief. Today, I will search to find my voice, and once I

have found it, I will seek to inspire others to find their voices. Today, I will value those crucial conversations I have with others and will grasp the golden opportunities to impart wisdom on others.

3. *Today*, I will reinforce belief in myself and in others. Today, I will understand that confidence is the memory of success, and success can only be achieved through consistent, repetitive practice. Today, I will affirm and validate the worth and potential in myself and in others. I will seek to match my internal thoughts with my external actions. Today, I will see people for what they can become rather than what they are. Today, I will not judge, compare, criticize, complain, contend, or fall victim to complacency on my journey of improvement. Today, I will illuminate the positive in others versus the negative.

4. *Today*, I will understand that a whole person is made up of four parts: body, mind, heart, and spirit. Today, when I use this whole-person paradigm, I will understand that to build up another I will have to pay them fairly (for the body), use them creatively (for the mind), treat them kindly (for the heart), and help them connect to meaning and source (for the spirit). Today, I will not neglect one dimension but will search for the complete picture and will use the whole-person paradigm as an accurate source to diagnose and predict the challenges we face in the world. Today, I will understand that each of these four parts produces four unique needs: to live (for the body), to learn (for the mind), to love (for the heart), and to leave a legacy (for the spirit). Once I grasp this concept, I will better utilize my voice in helping others to find their voices.

5. *Today*, I will seek to build up others and treat them solely from the perspective of their potential versus their weakness. Today, I will

help people believe and dream again. Today, I will offer hope through affirmation, validation, appreciation, and motivation, and I will not use fear, power, or position to get another person to move in a certain direction.

6. *Today,* I will choose not to participate in any negativity. Today, I will defend those who are not present, or I will walk away from negative people who only seek the benefit of themselves at the expense of another. Today, I will choose to operate from a perspective of positive energy and goodness versus negative energy and wasted time. Today, I will not allow others to define who I am or where I am going. Today, I will not be concerned with social status but rather with aligning my life with correct principles that benefit the greater good. Today, I will remain positive even as life challenges me.

7. *Today,* I will seek the benefit of others first versus my own benefit. Today, I will seek to trade paradigms with another versus judging, criticizing, or downgrading another person. Today, I will search for third alternatives to challenges versus becoming emotional and stuck in old, outdated ways of finding answers that rely on a formal position. Today, I will think outside the box rather than remain stagnant and still. Today, I will be dynamic and will seek to become the change I wish to see in the world. Today, I will practice the three key strategies for building others up and will not participate in needless drama.

Chapter 8

Act or Be Acted Upon

"We run our day or our day runs us."

—*Jim Rohn*

THE PROCESS OF WRITING this book has been a long and exhilarating journey. Today, I chose to take up space at a lake in Nashville, Tennessee, to finish work on this chapter, which centers on possibly the most important concept of the book: action. As I sit on a park bench and look out over Percy Priest Lake, I am overwhelmed with emotion and passion. Just yesterday I spoke at a men's breakfast and shared with a small group my belief that one can live inspired daily, make a significant contribution to the greater good, and live a life of deep meaning and passionate execution by practicing these seven simple decisions.

Easily the largest execution gap in America is an inability to act, an inability to translate thought into action. For some reason, there are a variety of variables that affect people's ability to take a stimulus and turn it into reality. This problem is epidemic across the country, and I think it stems from an imbalance in the four dimensions of body, mind, heart, and spirit. For too long, people have simply settled for a life of mediocrity and average accomplishments. We have a choice daily to become great. Each day we choose which road we will take. As Stephen Covey said, one road is the broad, well-traveled road to mediocrity that straightjackets human potential and self-worth. The other road is the road less traveled, which is the road to greatness and meaning. For some reason we can create a better vision in our heads, but we do not have the fortitude to make that thought part of who we are.

I have seen countless people who so desperately want a better life. They are discouraged and distressed and are looking for something that can profoundly affect their lives. I believe that something can be found in simplicity. As you finish this challenge I encourage you to live daily, to learn continuously, to love abundantly, and to leave a legacy for all those who will follow. The biggest person we need to lead every day is ourselves.

You Always Have a Choice

One of the most important concepts that a person can ever understand is the concept of stimulus and response. Between what happens to you and how you respond is a space. In that space lies your ability and power to choose your response. This space is also present between thinking and doing, and unfortunately this is where the largest gap in the world exists—the infamous execution gap. In *Decision No. 2: Design Your Own Dream,* I asked you to live out of your imagination instead of your memory and not to allow your past to hold your future hostage. That aspect is the first step of taking something from thought to reality. The second creation is in the action, the doing. If you realize that you are ultimately responsible for the success or failure of your life between your stimulus and response, you act.

Projecting blame on to others, being a victim of circumstance or past scripting, or making excuses for not executing only causes you to lose the private battles of your life, handcuffing and stifling your credibility with yourself and others. You simply have to grasp the concept that you always have a choice in how you respond, and within that choice lies the seeds of fruition or merely concepts of discussion. I think it is important for you to visually see what that space might look like so you have an idea of what to look for when you experience this process.

Stimulus and Response: The Gap

Stimulus ➡ Response

As you can see, between what happens to you or between you having a thought and manifesting that thought lies this space. Proactive people use this space wisely by cultivating the self-discipline and capacity to act. Unmotivated and reactive people simply breakdown in that space and cannot complete the thought or action. This leads to an enormous disconnect within one's conscience and is a major contributor to low trust levels with others. Remember this simple observation: People believe what you do, not what you say. If you cannot span this gap, it is most likely because you have not developed the much-needed capacity to do so by first making and keeping commitments to yourself. Daily private victories will lead to increased public victories as well as an inward and outward confidence.

Victor Frankl (1997) in *Man's Search for Meaning* said that the last and most precious freedom that individuals possess is the power and freedom to choose. While in a Nazi concentration camp, Frankl lost almost everything he had—except his ability to decide how he handled the adversity around him. From that experience he defined an individual's ability to choose as "our last human freedom." Your choice is between your stimulus (a thought or an external event) and your response (action taken from that thought or as a result of that event). Proactive people realize that in that space between stimulus and response they always, always have a choice. Reactive people lack the self-discipline and capacity to act between their thoughts and actions and allow the actions of others to define them in ways they do not like. Proactive people possess the creative factors of their life and do not empower the weaknesses of others to control them.

When you understand that you have the power to choose, you realize that you control how you respond in every situation that will ever happen to you in your life. You are let out of prison by others who seek to define you by the social mirror, status, money, house, clothes, ability, or comparing and competing for your sense of self-worth with others. This is liberating and emancipating and will help you take full responsibility for your moods, thoughts, and feelings. This realization will free you from becoming dependent on others for your internal happiness.

As situations happen that you are not comfortable with, you have the ability to suspend thought and action in this space until you have the knowledge, skills, desire, or beliefs that you need to act in ways that are congruent with your true mission, which is the ultimate goal. Translating your espoused or internal mission to the moments of your life will create a dynamic feeling of congruence, meaning, and purpose. This will connect you to your spirit just as I have been throughout the writing of this book. Remember the concept between inspiration and motivation? One is where the idea has a hold on you, and the other is where you have a hold on the idea. We should seek to place ourselves in places where we can become inspired, because inspirational things happen in inspirational settings.

When you are building the emotional strength to act, think of doing twenty emotional push-ups. The practice helps you build the capacity to act when needed. If you fail to cultivate the internal strength to meet the external challenges, you will not be able to connect the mission to the moment, and this will leave you feeling frustrated and intimidated by life and what others throw your way. The most important concept to understand is that you have the capacity to meet these challenges once you move from a reactionary stance toward a proactive stance. Now you just need to build the important ingredient: capacity.

Build Your Capacity to Act

When you understand that you have the power to make anything happen and the power to choose your response to virtually any situation, you must next understand how to build the internal self-discipline to convert thought into action. There are a variety of factors that prohibit individuals from conversion, but some that I've witnessed include:

- fear of failure
- fear of embarrassment
- activity traps of life
- entrenched, old ways of acting
- deeply embedded failure mind-sets
- too difficult
- too much work
- culture won't permit any change
- fear of change
- fear of uncertainty

If you have allowed any of these excuses to permeate your life and prohibit you from acting on your mental thought processes, you have held yourself hostage in a self-contained prison. Deep within each us is a longing, a hunger for meaning and contribution, a need to find our voices in life and make a difference.

In a recent study, a fear of not making a difference in life ranked higher than a fear of death. Why then do we allow the factors that we can control to lock us out from realizing our potential in this world?

The answer is simple. The lack of self-discipline to connect our mission to the moments of our lives straightjackets our potential and pushes us into a life of default versus a life of design. How do we build this capacity? We complete twenty emotional push-ups.

THE TWENTY EMOTIONAL PUSH-UPS

Just as there is an emotional bank account (Covey, 1989) with others where the currency is trust, there is a personal emotional bank account for which we have to make deposits for ourselves. This is where private victories are won that develop our capacity to convert thoughts into actions and win public victories in the eyes of society. Here are several ways to build your capacity to meet the challenge of creating action around your thoughts:

1. Make and keep commitments to yourself.
2. Set goals and objectives and attain them.
3. Educate and obey your conscience by living from principles.
4. Plan, execute, then reflect for improvement.
5. Translate your deep internal mission into an emotionally charged situation.
6. Forgive others who transgress against you.
7. Become a light that illuminates the good in others.
8. Be loyal to those who are absent.
9. Do not use formal authority to bully someone into having your way.
10. Seek first the benefit of others versus your own benefit.
11. Move away from justifying your point when others disagree.
12. Lose pride and ego. Both will cause you to make very poor decisions.
13. Practice not judging others.

14. Reflect on your internal dialogue and change it to positive thoughts.
15. Do not assume motive when dealing with others.
16. Live in the present, plan for the future, learn from the past.
17. Plan and execute time to reflect, exercise, educate yourself, and plan.
18. Learn to build others up (including yourself) rather than tear them down.
19. Believe and practice abundance.
20. Build confidence through little victories.

As you can see, you build capacity by doing. Confidence is the memory of success, and you become successful by constant repetition. Only through a consistent buildup of skills and knowledge do you garner the capacity to act in tough situations in your life. To get there you must first identify the things that are limiting this process. Many are emotional cancers that create a stalemate in your life that you simply lack the energy to act.

How do you build capacity to act in your work, your physical training, with your children, or with various projects in your life? You practice, right? You can only build the capacity to act in your life through consistent, repetitive action and experience. This process begins with winning private victories. Just as I noted earlier, you must win the private victory daily so you can win the public victory later. You build capacity to act by educating your mind and your heart, by constantly expanding your horizons, by growing your knowledge and skills, and by growing your desire and your beliefs. This sequential, integrated process begins by growing in four dimensions described earlier:

1. **For the mind:** Grow your knowledge through expansion, challenge, reading, and sharing knowledge and ideas.

2. **For the body:** Grow your health through regular exercise, a healthy diet, proper rest, and maintaining and challenging yourself to grow stronger.
3. **For the heart:** Grow your passion through participating in causes you in which you believe deeply, not being judgmental of others, forgiving those who have wronged you, loving, and by being passionate about your vocation.
4. **For the spirit:** Grow your conscience by making and keeping commitments to yourself and others, practicing regular reflection and renewal, spending time with nature, expressing your voice through your job, cultivating and connecting to your source, and practicing living with an open heart and mind.

You grow your capacity to act just as you would grow your capacity to lift weights. Start with the twenty emotional push-ups by translating your mission into a trying moment in your life, verbalizing something with both courage and consideration (a sign of maturity), and by making and keeping a commitment about which you have strong feelings. As you grow this capacity you will begin to live in alignment with what matters most to you, and this congruence will light a fire in you that others will notice.

Now, we must identify the roadblocks that may impede you from finding your voice and building your capacity. Remember, when we engage in new behaviors in a systematic manner, it allows us to do things tomorrow that we could never do today and that is what we want.

IDENTIFY THE ROADBLOCKS

There are six emotional cancers. Stephen Covey defined five of the six, but the sixth is my own. First, it is important to outline what cancer is. In *Presence,* Peter Senge (2004) defined this type of cancer by observing, "A cell that loses its social identity reverts to blind undifferentiated cell division, which can ultimately threaten the life of the larger organism." Many people unfortunately have developed functional blind spots to the cancers they have allowed to manifest in their lives, therefore leading them to operate from an inaccurate and fragmented paradigm. Until they can see that they are emotionally connected or practice this cancerous behavior, they continue to wander aimlessly in life, blaming and reacting to the short end of the stick they constantly subscribe to.

As I noted in the beginning of the book, you must stop and reflect on what is happening in your life to see if you are getting the results you want. If not, you could be affected by one of the following six cancers.

- *Complaining:* A spirit of reactiveness that suggests you have no control over your situation, so you will make everyone aware of your misery in an effort to manipulate them into massaging your heart. This is enormously unhelpful and wastes valuable energy toward trying to solve whatever it is you are experiencing. Ask yourself this question, "Has whining, pouting, moping, or blaming someone about a situation ever produced any positive outcomes?" If not, then stop.

- *Comparing:* When you compare yourself to others or the social mirror, you are operating from a scarcity mind-set. People are different for a reason, and every person brings unique talents to the table. Getting into who is more popular, who wears the nicest clothes, who is prettier, who lives in the biggest house, or who has the most money are reactive behaviors that rob us of our own uniqueness. The social mirror is a powerful script but also a lousy one. Once you find your voice in life, you won't be so concerned with social status but more attuned to what you are really doing with your life. Immature people compare themselves to others. Mature people value diversity and seek to see the beauty in all people, including their own.

- *Contending:* Carrying a contentious spirit or negativity everywhere you go is highly reactive. You have one life. How you handle the daily challenges of that life determines your quality of life. Becoming negative, cynical, combative, or defensive makes you look back and produces a profound misalignment with your inner conscience. You will feel this misalignment and know deep down that you have more to offer the world than a negative spirit.

- *Criticizing:* Criticizing others stems from a viewpoint of control, fear, insecurity, and scarcity. When we criticize others we look weak, and our criticism only promotes a dependence on the social mirror. There's a reason we learned at an early age, "If you can't say something nice about someone, don't say anything at all." Think about how others look when they criticize. Remember, "If you want to retain those who are present, be loyal to those who are absent."

- *Competing:* When we compete internally against those we should be working with or against the social mirror for our own sense of self-worth, we simply lose. As a coach, I understand the value of competing, but my basic belief is that cooperation far exceeds competition in the long run. I have been in workplace situations where everyone competed for support, value, time, space, and ego. These situations always led to lose-lose outcomes, and the individuals competing

174

could not see that the wedge they used to supposedly win in the short term only caused them to lose in the long term. Value yourself and what you have to offer and value others around you. Cooperate internally and compete externally. Value your competition as your best teacher, not your worst enemy.

- *Complacency:* I added this emotional cancer to Covey's first five because I believe that complacency is an important killer. The cancer of complacency assumes you have arrived and sets in when we become content with our current situation and have experienced some level of success. Many times I have witnessed individuals climb the ladder of success with passion, patience, persistence, and perseverance only to stagnate, plateau, and lose the ferocity it took to get there. This is a very sad situation in all facets of life. Life's journey is filled with peaks and valleys, and we only gain experience and knowledge by occasionally losing. We should constantly evaluate and reflect on what works and what does not and be on fire to learn and grow. Our unique human endowments of self-awareness and imagination allow us to recreate ourselves constantly in new and better ways and to grow daily as we experience new learning. Don't allow yourself to become complacent in life and just stay where you are. Complacency is a reactive stance, but it usually stems from a disconnect from the source of passion or an event that dispirits the soul in such a way that you lose hope. This all derives from viewing people from the holistic perspective I've mentioned throughout this book. If you break someone's spirit hard enough, do not be surprised if they lose faith in the mission of the organization and withdraw into complacency while they look for other people who value what they have to offer. The same is true in interpersonal relationships with others.

EAT AN ELEPHANT ONE BITE AT A TIME

Unfortunately, many people want what they want when they want it, which is right now. Reflecting on my coaching and leadership career, I can see the small, incremental steps I took to get where I am today. I can remember coaching at a small elementary school in the beginning when I worked for $199.50 for two years. At that point in my life, it was the biggest thing I could be doing, and I understood the concept introduced earlier: every day at your current job is an interview for your future job. You see, people are always watching and observing, and it's clear to see which individuals are driven by the expression of their voices through vision, discipline, passion, and conscience. The individuals who build an enormous reservoir of knowledge and talent in specific areas will eventually find and plug into an outlet and into the people they need in order to materialize their dreams.

There are a few important concepts to grasp when it comes to turning thought into action:

1. You must first understand that your time is valuable, and what you do with it affects the quality of your life. Your time is an investment, and you choose what you want to invest in.
2. You must understand that creating a vision for your life is one of the easiest parts. Many people talk a lot about what they could become, but they never do anything about it.
3. You must learn to believe in your ability, cultivate a large knowledge base, and grow your capacity to act versus only converse.
4. Once you understand the power of the spirit and the power of conscience in driving your actions when you have found your voice, nothing will stop you from achieving what you set out to do.

5. Goals are the most overused, underdone concept in America. Work from the four-dimensional approach to cultivate these capacities in the realization of your goals.

- Mind—Vision—Imagination
- Body—Discipline—Execution
- Heart—Passion—Fuel
- Spirit—Conscience—Connection to Meaning

Once you find your voice at these intersections and balance these four intelligences and capacities, you will begin to live fully, love completely, learn daily, and seek to leave a legacy in both your organization and your life. This will produce action around your vision. Remember, start small with daily private victories. This could include not being judgmental today or simply going an entire day without being negative toward another. Small daily private victories will lead to large public victories. Where you are on the emotional maturity continuum will determine where you are and where you need to go.

HAVE A MISSION AND CONNECT THAT
MISSION TO EVERY MOMENT

Once you develop a mission that you believe in, emotionally identify with, and walk through the process of understanding stimulus and response, you are ready to translate your mission into the tough moments of your life. This will allow you the power and freedom to act in ways that are deeply aligned with your inner voice and create actions around your highest priorities. Many people believe that mission statements are soft and mushy, but the reality of the situation is that, if used properly, they become a powerful guiding force and constitution for your life. Most of the people who don't believe mission statements work have not built their own capacity to act; they put up defensive mechanisms that allow them to fail before they even get started. This is my mission statement:

PASSION—PERSISTENCE—PATIENCE—PERSERVERANCE
To live fully,
To influence many,
To learn daily,
To love without judgment,
To leave a legacy for those who follow,
To think big,
To act on those thoughts,
To help others detect their passion and reach their potential,
To model maturity and wisdom,
To forgive those who have transgressed against me,
To be a Difference Maker,
To sacrifice for the greater good,
To continue to seek guidance and spirituality,
To live a life that matters,
To give glory to our creator, and
To live like I were dying!

As you can see I placed four words at the top of my mission statement. My good friend and mentor Bill McEwen shared those with me as part of his own mission statement. This is the fuel that drives the car. Everyone needs passion to get where they are going. It rows your boat and brings an unwavering desire to see something through to the end. Persistence is the ability to keep going despite opposition, dispirited events, naysayers, and things outside your circle of control. Patience must be displayed in all facets of life. God has a plan for each of us but not always according to our timetable. Just as nature acts in harmony and on its own timetable, so too does the human life cycle. Patience is very much a virtue that must be cultivated. Wherever you are, remember, be fully present in the moment and understand that everything is exactly as it should be at the time. Perseverance is the emotional intelligence component that is a necessity to be successful in today's fast-paced world. It is the ability to bounce back from adversity when you get knocked down, the ability to be self-intrinsically motivated, the ability to be compassionate to others, and the ability to work through challenge to thrive.

Once you have cultivated your own mission statement, it is necessary to live that mission statement. Think about how many times you see a mission statement in an organization that proclaims one thing (such as unmatched customer service) only to get the exact opposite. If you do this in your own personal life you will create so much static internally that it will limit you from finding your voice in life and will urge you to keep others from finding their voices. This internal turmoil will cause you grief and misalignment with your conscience and will stagnate your life.

Mission statements, if produced properly, tap into your heart, mind, and soul and should be sacred documents that tie thoughts with actions. If you produced this document it makes an imprint on your brain and helps you make it legitimate in your heart. As you live from your mission statement, you are connecting what you feel is important to the many challenges of your life.

When you begin connecting the dots from your deeply held beliefs to your daily transactions with others, a deep wellspring of peace and simplicity will take over your life, and you will begin to understand that all people are connected to the same source. Now that you have five important components in place, it's time for an important breakthrough in your life. Something is building inside you, and you are about to experience a powerful awakening.

MOMENTUM IS YOUR GREATEST FRIEND

As you continue to build the capacity to act through consistent, repetitive actions, you begin to see positive things manifesting in your life, both intentionally and mysteriously. You experience what Jim Collins (*Good to Great,* 2001) described as Build Up and Breakthrough. At many times you have probably seen the fruits of your labor because intentional actions manifested positive things in your life. But surprisingly, many of the good things in your life are simply a by-product of a series of good, principle-centered decisions that gradually build up over time. This series of good decisions comes from a deep knowing of one's inner self and an awareness and "presencing" that operate inside you when you believe and act in harmony with your deepest core.

I have experienced this in my own life, when good things happened as a result of continuing to practice the belief model of believing, seeing, doing, and reflecting. Reflection in the process is critical for long-term success, because it cultivates the self-awareness necessary to bring about change. It is also vitally important to gain momentum with your decisions by acting around your highest priorities. Without execution, dreams stay in the concept stage and never become reality. Many visionaries see grandeur images of a better world, a better life, and a better company, but they fail to execute those visions.

Peter Senge (*Presence,* 2004) quoted Robert Fritz: "Building the capacity to crystallize a larger intent requires daily practice, working with what he calls structural tension. This 'structural tension' requires crystallizing vision and recognizing present reality and is especially useful in times of stress or daily crises." The structural and creative tension in your life are the necessary ingredients to spur you to act on what you envision.

As your four dimensions are optimized in the pursuit of greatness, you begin to see that you have a deep calling or purpose in life.

Senge noted, "What matters is engagement in the service of a larger purpose rather than lofty actions that paralyze action."

We expect success to happen overnight. We see pictures of movie stars that have it all. What we don't see is the road each of them took and where they came from to achieve that level of success. The real success is in the doing, in the journey, and in the acting around one's priorities. As you move in the direction of your dreams with intention, that very intention will co-create your reality. Begin building up today because you are well on your way to a breakthrough soon. Now is the time to create your ultimate mission statement: live like you were dying.

LIVE LIKE YOU WERE DYING

When you create a mission statement, it needs to become a powerful, living document that is a personal constitution for how you want to live your life. Too often we simply allow others to define us or circumstances to control us or we disempower ourselves and allow the world to hold us hostage. We have forgotten how to dream and take control of our lives, our time, our energy, and our future. As we become older we begin to understand that time is the most precious commodity we will ever have. We cherish the little things, forget the silly things, and seek to serve and uplift others. We answer a calling to a higher purpose, and we see the beauty in virtually everything we do, even amid adversity.

Tim McGraw, one of my favorite singers, recently released the song "Live Like You Were Dying." Many people have made that statement often, but in that particular context it made sense to me. I began to close my speaking engagements by challenging everyone to value every second, every minute, every hour, and every day in an upward spiral of service, meaning, and contribution. I challenged everyone to live like they were dying. Today, for you it may be to let go of some hurt you've harbored, forgive someone who has hurt you, quit allowing the past to hold your future hostage, stop allowing others to define who you are and what you stand for, quit the job you hate, tell the one you love, be there for someone who needs you, enjoy a moment of peace, practice spirituality, or make a conscious choice to be thankful, humble, and happy.

I don't know where you are on your journey, but I will assume yours is not that much different than mine: full of hope, passion, dreams, sorrow, joy, and abundant opportunity. What you personally decide to do between stimulus and response will make all the difference in the world as it relates to your living a life that matters. From my perspective, the most powerful mission statement in the world is to live like you were dying.

Four Key Points from Ninety-Five-Year-Olds

They did a study of ninety-five-year-old people who were about to pass this earth. They asked them if they could go back and live again, what would be some key advice they would live by. You might take want to incorporate some of this advice in your life:

1. We only get one life, but if we work it just right, one is all you will ever need. Never put off until tomorrow what you can and should do today.
2. When our lives are over, we will far more regret what we could have done and should have done versus what we actually did. Minimize regret by acting now.
3. Life is a contact sport. We advance by losing ourselves in service to others.
4. Life is a series of small and big moments. Make those moments matter and never let your years get in the way of your moments.

Chapter 8 Summary: Seven Action Items to Manifest the Decision of Act or Be Acted Upon

1. *Today,* I will fully understand that between stimulus (what happens to me) and my response (how I choose to respond) is a space, and in that space lies my ability to choose my response. Today, I will accept full responsibility for how I feel, what I think, how I choose to act, and what I do. Today, I will build the important capacity and overcome the hardwiring of my past and the cultural software of my present and seek to become a person of trustworthiness, influence, change, and positive energy. Today, I will manage my energy and place it in areas that leverage my talents and passions so that it has the most dramatic impact on society and my organization.

2. *Today,* I will fully understand that building internal strength is like building external strength. Today, I will lift the internal weights of making and keeping my commitments to others and myself. Today, I will educate and obey my conscience by living a principle-centered life. Today, I will act in my moments of choice to translate my mission to the daily tough points of my life. Today, I will seek to create a synergy between my walk and my talk, and I will act in congruence with my inner self. Today, I will practice abundance versus scarcity and be genuinely pleased for the success of others. Today, I will not say a negative word about another behind their back, and I will practice patience and humility. Today, I will build rather than destroy.

3. *Today,* I will practice self-awareness to identify my personal road-blocks. I will re-imagine, re-create, and re-connect with who I am and where I want to go. Today, there will be no mistaken identity of my true character, because I will seek to illuminate the good in

others by what I radiate. Today, I will recognize the six emotional cancers of comparing, contending, competing, criticizing, complaining, and complacency. Today, I will build a strong internal immune system by not participating or allowing any emotional cancer to spread in me or throughout my organization. Today, I will be light, not a judge. Today, I will be a model, not a critic. Today, I will overcome each of my perceived roadblocks and work daily to grow, expand, and mature.

4. *Today,* I will ask, "What one action can I take with a singleness of purpose and intention that will leverage the most return on my investment of time and will have the most positive impact on me and the organizations I associate with?" Today, I will seek to build the twenty emotional push-ups so I can garner the internal strength to meet the external challenges. Today, I will place my time and my energy in causes and people I deem worthy, and I will seek to leave this world and the people in it better than I found them. Today, I will focus on my circle of influence to grow that circle, and I will start small and achievable. Every step I take will be in the direction of my dreams. Today, I will believe in myself and in my causes, and I will seek to improve both.

5. *Today,* I will translate my mission into the moments of my life. Today, I will seek to live inspired by tapping into my natural birth gifts of body, mind, heart, and spirit. Today, I will live in congruence with my mission in life, and I will work to embody goodness. Today, I will not allow my environment or what others think of me to define who I am or what I do. Today, I will build the internal security to act in my tough moments of my private life. Today, I will seek to win the private battles of my life so I can win the public battles. Today, I will become the change I seek to create in the world.

6. *Today,* I will understand that momentum is my friend and companion. I will work to create momentum in all phases of my life. Today, I will work with a purpose, fervor, intention, and passion toward a worthy cause that I believe in. Today, I will no longer put off until tomorrow what I could do today. Today, I will act between my stimulus and response. Today, I will continue to build, knowing that the more I build the more I will receive. Today, I will detach myself from outcomes and only focus on the process, knowing that outcomes will take care of themselves. Today, I will think and act in new ways to achieve new levels of success and significance.

7. *Today,* I will live like I were dying. Today, I will value life. Today, I will value people. Today, I will use my God-given talents to enrich the world. Today, I will lose myself in service to others. Today, I will laugh, smile, sing, dance, listen, help, restore, reconnect, rejuvenate, reimagine, and practice renewal in my life. Today, I will work in all dimensions to grow myself and others. Today, I will become the person I set out to become. Today, I will experience an awakening, design my own dream, learn to play up, make learning a way of being, add value versus subtract it, build up versus tear down, and act versus be acted upon. Today, I will work from the end picture in my mind of my life and take the important advice and wisdom of those who have gone before me. Today, I will live to my fullest potential and offer the world my best self.

Afterword

THE JOURNEY OF COMPLETING this book began more than five years ago. It speaks to the power of manifestation in your life when you have something so strong on the inside that it seeks so desperately to come out. Since writing the first edition of this book I have given the message around these core decisions to over 125,000 people all around the country and taught the material in every class I've ever been in. These decisions become habits in your life and serve as the blueprint and guideposts to help you reach your deepest potential. In essence, the beginning of this journey signified the beginning point of my finding my voice in life and working to inspire others to find their voices.

The seeds of this book were planted one day while speaking in a class at Middle Tennessee State University (where I earned my first two degrees) when it came to me what I really wanted to say. That day I begin to call my topic "This Ain't No Practice Life." Deep within each of us is a longing to matter, to contribute, to execute, and to be involved in moving the world forward. Sometimes we become reactive, we fail to recognize how our contributions matters, we lose our voice or become frustrated with the process, so we just stay where we are. In reality there is no just staying where we are. We either focus on the solution or we become part of the problem.

By staying stagnant, we actively participate in the mediocrity of the world. As Gandhi said, "We must become the change we seek to create in the world." The seven keys that I have put together are common sense but not always common practice. They will help you work in a sequential, integrated process toward improving your quality of life, both personally and professionally.

The enormous growth that has taken place inside me as a result of sharing this message across the United States has been profound. I believe that these decisions will help you begin the process that will help you to play at a different level in life. Each step of the way I have illustrated how they have affected me personally to show you that it is possible with everyone. I grew up from a small-town boy in Woodbury, Tennessee, to be an accomplished coach, author, entrepreneur, speaker, and thought leader.

Dr. Wayne Dyer (*The Power of Intention,* 2004) noted when he wrote daily, the words came to him from his source or his connection to spirit. I did not fully understand that process until I wrote this book. Each word emanates from my deepest being and my connection to my spirit. There is a strong push for spiritual intelligence in America today. To me, this is illustrated through the whole-person paradigm of body, mind, heart, and spirit. To work toward your own self-actualization and self-transcendence, you must first find your voice in life by experiencing the awakening I speak of in this book, followed by a period of designing your dreams. This will be followed with the sequential processes of learning to play up, making learning a way of being, and adding value rather than subtracting it. Once you are there, you will begin to build others up and act rather than being acted upon by the world.

My goal for you is simple: live an inspired life and search to create everyday greatness. Deep within each of us is the seed of uniqueness. We are charged with the responsibility of finding and detecting our contribution to the particular needs of the world, and then fulfilling that need with our talent and passion as we are driven by our conscience. God bless each and every one of you for taking this journey. My heart goes out to all of those who accepted the fact that this ain't no practice life.

Now, go make the world a better place!

Bibliography

Bennett-Goleman, T. (2001). *Emotional Alchemy: How the Mind Can Heal the Heart.* New York: Harmony Books.

Chopra, D. (1994). *The Seven Spiritual Laws of Success: A Practical Guide to the Fulfillment of Your Dreams.* San Rafael, CA: Amber-Allen Publishing.

Collins, J. (2001). *Good to Great: Why Some Companies Make the Leap—And Others Don't.* San Francisco: HarperCollins.

Covey, S. (1989). *The Seven Habits of Highly Effective People: Restoring the Character Ethic.* New York: Simon and Shuster.

Covey, S. (2004). *The 8th Habit: From Effectiveness to Greatness.* New York: Free Press.

Dyer, W. (2004). *The Power of Intention: Learning to Co-Create Your World Your Way.* Carlsbad, CA: Hay House Inc.

Frankl, V. (1997). *Man's Search for Meaning: An Introduction to Logotherapy.* Boston: Beacon Press.

Friedman, T. (2006). *The World Is Flat: A Brief History of the Twenty-First Century.* New York: Farrar, Straus, and Giroux.

Kouzes, J., and Posner, B. (2002). *The Leadership Challenge.* 3rd ed. San Francisco: Wiley.

Kuhn, T. (1962). *The Structure of Scientific Revolutions.* Chicago: University of Chicago Press.

Mackay, H. (2004). *We Got Fired! And It's the Best Thing That Ever Happened to Us.* New York: Ballantine Books.

Mandino, Og. (1968). *The Greatest Salesman in the World.* New York: Frederick Fell Publishers Inc.

Maxwell, J. C. (2000). *Developing the Leader Within You.* Nashville: Thomas Nelson.

Senge, P., et al. (2004). *Presence: Human Purpose and the Field of the Future.* Cambridge, MA: Society for Organizational Learning.

Wilkinson, B. (2009). *You Were Born for This: Seven Keys to a Life of Predictable Miracles.* Colorado Springs: Multnomah Books.

Check out all things Micheal Burt at www.coachburt.com.
Listen weekly to *The Coach Micheal Burt Radio Show*
on www.wlac.com.

About Coach Micheal Burt

COACH MICHEAL BURT IS a leader to leaders, consulting and coaching some of the top performers and organizations in the country on how to find their unique abilities, enhance their leadership skills, close the gaps in execution, and build cultures that produce again and again. Don't you think it's time to partner with someone who knows how to produce results at the highest levels?

Coach Burt is quickly being recognized as THE leadership expert in Tennessee, and he continues to grow his message regionally to attract nationally. Currently, Coach Burt and Dr. Colby Jubenville, the strategist, focus on personal growth, leadership, manifesting dreams, building cultures that win, and playing at a different level. Few shows in the country provide an hour of positive energy that really addresses the hard issues of life and the battles we all face individually and collectively.

The show can be heard Sundays at 12:00 p.m. on www.wlac.com.

"You're one phone call away from changing your life." Partnering with Nashville-based DBR Media, Coach Burt focuses on steady growth to connect his message to a larger audience each month.

Coach Burt is also founder and CEO of Maximum Success, the marketing and publishing division of CoachBurt.com. At Maximum Success, we believe a brand is a promise that is delivered through an experience. We employ a unique and innovative systems-based marketing approach that focuses on the relationship between customers, organizations, and employees. We win and keep customers for your business. Micheal has worked with Dell Inc., State Farm Insurance, FirstBank, Ole South Properties, Middle Tennessee State University, the John C. Jones Real Estate Team, Kendra Cooke and Associates, Phil Cavender Financial, Reeves-Sain, Tennessee School Boards Association, the Tennessee Health Care Association, National Health Care, Farrer Brothers Construction, Miller, Loughry, and Beach, and many others.

About CoachBurt.com and Maximum Success

MAXIMUM SUCCESS, a division of CoachBurt.com, is a multimedia strategy company that focuses on comprehensive systems for recruitment, retention, and growth that create a unique experience for employees, managers, and customers. Our unique training and consultancy programs seek to tap into each part of an individual's nature to educate the mind, value the heart, reward the body, and stimulate the spirit. Based on the unique processes cultivated by coachepreneur Micheal Burt, Maximum Success offers the outsourcing of branding and positioning, multimedia and Web development, leadership and sales management, and culture building around the concept of speed and integration. With the help of Dr. Colby Jubenville, the strategist and chief consultant to Coach Burt, multimedia specialist Ernie Gray, and other specialty skilled entrepreneurs, Maximum Success puts a world-class team on the floor every time.

Maximum Success builds cultures that consistently win by creating loyalty within organizations, delivering exciting experiences to employees, management, and customers, and creating a brand-delivery approach that permeates every aspect of a company.

Maximum Success has found that most organizations do not focus on systems for recruitment and retention of their greatest assets: great employees. This is due to a misalignment and lack of understanding of basic human nature. To motivate and inspire people to offer their whole self to an organization, we must first understand that people consist of body, mind, heart, and spirit. Most companies fail to recognize that what they really want from each employee is their whole self and for motivation to be internal and voluntary. Based on Coach Burt's unique experiences as a championship coach and a deep entrepreneurial education, he is able to drive major results within companies and improve profits as well as culture.

Maximum Success and Coach Burt have spoken to or worked with the following organizations to help drive a culture that consistently wins in the market: Dell Inc., State Farm Insurance, National Health Care, FirstBank, Reeves-Sain, Ole South Properties, John Jones Real Estate, Kendra Cooke and Associates, SouthBranch, Quality Landscaping, and Miller, Loughry, and Beach Insurance (a division of Pinnacle).

Coach Micheal Burt's philosophy of leading Maximum Success centers around a holistic approach by which you lead people and manage things around four core values: voice, leadership, execution, and culture.

As one of the fastest growing leadership consulting firms in the Southeast, with plans to become a global training and development center, Maximum Success is headquartered in Murfreesboro, Tennessee, and can be reached by phone at (615) 225-8380, online at www.maximumsuccess.org, or by e-mailing Coach Burt directly at coachburt@maximumsuccess.org.

TO BOOK COACH BURT TO SPEAK AT YOUR NEXT EVENT

Coach Burt speaks on the titles of each of his books with a special focus in leadership, personal motivation, sales, and building cultures that consistently WIN. Looking for a powerful keynote, half-day training session, or a full day that will transform your life, then call Coach Burt today.

To book Coach Burt by e-mail, contact the strategist, Dr. Colby Jubenville, at colby@coachburt.com

Coach Micheal Burt is a leader to leaders, consulting and coaching some of the top performers and organizations in the country on how to find their unique abilities, enhance their leadership skills, close the gaps in execution, and build cultures that produce again and again. Don't you think it's time to partner with someone who knows how to produce results at the highest levels?

LISTEN TO COACH BURT ON CHANGE YOUR LIFE RADIO

One hour. One phone call. Listen to Change Your Life Radio with Coach Micheal Burt and the strategist, Dr. Colby Jubenville!

Everybody needs a coach in life. Isn't it time you found yours?

Coach Burt is recognized as THE leadership expert in Tennessee and continues to grow his message regionally to attract a national audience. Coach Burt and Dr. Colby Jubenville, the strategist, focus on personal growth, leadership, manifesting dreams, building cultures that win, and playing at a different level. Few radio shows in the country provide an hour of positive energy that really addresses the hard issues of life and the battles we all face individually and collectively.

The show can be heard Sundays at 12:00 p.m. on WLAC 1510 AM in Tennessee or nationally at www.wlac.com.

To be a part of the conversation, local listeners can call in by phone at (615) 737-9522 and national listeners can call in at 1-800-688-9522. Verizon Wireless subscribers can dial *9522.

You're one phone call away from changing your life.

Partnering with Nashville-based DBR Media, Coach Burt is focused on steady growth to connect his message to a larger audience each month. Micheal is also the leadership and personal growth expert featured every morning at 6:20 a.m. on SuperTalk Radio 99.7 WTN.

NOTES

NOTES

NOTES

NOTES

NOTES

NOTES

NOTES